THE ZEN OF
YOU & ME

Also by Diane Musho Hamilton

Everything Is Workable: A Zen Approach to Conflict Resolution (also available as an audiobook)

THE ZEN OF YOU & ME

*A Guide to Getting Along
with Just About Anyone*

DIANE MUSHO HAMILTON

SHAMBHALA
Boulder
2017

Shambhala Publications, Inc.
4720 Walnut Street
Boulder, Colorado 80301
www.shambhala.com

9 8 7 6 5 4 3 2 1
First Edition

Printed in the United States of America

♾ This edition is printed on acid-free paper that meets the
American National Standards Institute Z39.48 Standard.
♻ This book is printed on 30% post-consumer recycled paper.
For more information please visit www.shambhala.com.
Distributed in the United States by Penguin Random House LLC
and in Canada by Random House of Canada Ltd

Designed by Katrina Noble

Library of Congress Cataloging-in-Publication Data
Names: Musho Hamilton, Diane, author.
Title: The zen of you and me: a guide to getting along with
just about anyone / Diane Musho Hamilton.
Description: Boulder: Shambhala, 2017. | Includes
bibliographical references.
Identifiers: LCCN 2016028248 | ISBN 9781611803785 (paperback)
Subjects: LCSH: Mindfulness (Psychology) | Meditation. | Zen
Buddhism. | BISAC: BODY, MIND & SPIRIT / Meditation. |
RELIGION / Buddhism / Zen (see also PHILOSOPHY / Zen).
Classification: LCC BF637.M4 M87 2017 | DDC 158.2—dc23
LC record available at https://lccn.loc.gov/2016028248

Contents

Acknowledgments

I have been a student of the American writer and philosopher Ken Wilber for over fifteen years. He is an extraordinary man, a lover of unity and a genius in making fine, important distinctions. His work has changed my life and my work. If I can say so, he has always dumbed down his answers to meet me in my questions with such remarkable love and kindness; I am forever indebted to his generosity.

I want to thank Julia Sati for being the world's best assistant. Her devotional heart, intellectual precision, and outstanding midwestern work ethic have saved me in the beginning, the middle, and in the end. Deep gratitude to Rob McNamara, who if there are princes today is surely one. I have counted on him to always help me think the details through and give me the signal when to take it easy. I owe a big thank-you to Rebecca Colwell and the Ten Directions crew for their creative force and support of this work; to Brian Turner for his clarity, heart, and complete love of science; to Anita

Floris for suggesting I include "Harmony of Difference and Sameness"; to Jane Goetz for her beautiful edits. And to all my students for giving me the privilege of practicing and learning with them. They are risk takers, devotees of the Way, and true friends.

Thank you to the Zen ancestors, and particularly to my teacher, Genpo Roshi, for his dharma in all of its forms. Thank you to my parents for raising me with love and wide open room to be myself. And special gratitude to my husband, Michael, for seriously being who he is. Finally, I would like to thank David O'Neal at Shambhala Publications. It is a pleasure to work with someone I trust so much.

Preface

After Shambhala published my first book, *Everything Is Workable: A Zen Approach to Conflict Resolution*,[1] I was asked by an interested woman whether I would be writing a second one. I was like a mother with a tiny baby in her arms who is asked if she is planning to have a second child. The thought hadn't even occurred to me.

She went on to say that if I did write another book, it would be helpful if I focused less on conflict. "The word 'conflict' in the title," she said, "scares people away. Instead you should focus on skills that can help all relationships, even the good ones." She added, "I have a really good relationship with my mother, but I don't think we listen to each other very well. The relationship is good—as far as it goes."

"Good as far as it goes." I thought about that. What would it mean to write a book that helped people go a little further, even in their good relationships? I hesitated, thinking to myself that there are already so many good books written to support successful, wholesome relationships: intimacy books for couples, leadership books for executives and managers, and books for parents. I wasn't sure that I had anything more to add to this wide-ranging conversation. But the woman's phrase "good as far as it goes" played in my head.

It finally occurred to me that if I were to pick a subject that would help people go further, it would be an exploration of how we are the same and how we are different. I have been a mediator and a meditator for many years. In both domains, we bring "two into one." In meditation, the division is within ourselves—our ambivalence, struggles, and inner conflicts are relaxed on the cushion, and body, speech, and mind are experienced together. In mediation, the differences across the table are examined and explored. Two disputing parties create an agreement that binds them into one resolution. In practicing meditation or helping parties solve a problem, we must relate to the differences and work with them. But as the woman said, most of us just get along with the people we love. There is a built-in limit to our intimacy and trust because we shy away from acknowledging the true depth of our differences. Because it isn't simply that we are different. It is that our differences incur judgments: someone is better or worse; one person is right and the other person is wrong. To engage our differences is to engage our judgments, and our judgments usually pack an emotional punch, and that is where the difficulty begins.

I have practiced for years in meditation communities, and the emphasis on peace, commonality, and harmony provides a refuge for meditators and seekers on a path. The only problem is that when differences arise or conflicts erupt, people are often ill equipped to work with them. There is a tendency to view our differences as wrong, as somehow not "enlightened." When struggles persist, the whole spiritual enterprise becomes suspect. People then leave the practice disappointed. Sometimes the letdown feeds cynicism, and some people will never return.

This reluctance to explore differences doesn't just exist in our spiritual communities, but is everywhere. We experience these limits in our most intimate relationships. We have them with our friends, our colleagues, and neighbors who do things in a way that is unfamiliar, annoying, or alienating. I had a friend who once moved from his house because he didn't like the smell of his neighbor's cooking. Fair enough.

Sometimes the smell of someone else's fried fish is just too much at the end of a workday. But we can't escape the tiny and the vast differences between us—differences in race, religion, economic status, and even cuisine. These differences affect us every day on large and small scales, and because our brains and bodies are hardwired to interpret even slight variations between us as threatening, we have tremendous difficulty simply talking about them.

This book encourages us to open a conversation about difference. It is based on the assumption that the harmony that includes our differences is deeper and more durable than the one that doesn't. The book is written for those in relationships of all kinds: lovers and friends, married couples, coworkers and their managers, leaders and team members, teachers and students, parents and young people—anyone who is in a relationship, one that is "good as far as it goes," with the wish that by including our differences, we may deepen to a place of genuine unity.

SAME AND DIFFERENT

The mind of nirvana is easy to achieve.
It is the mind of difference that is difficult to attain.
—ZEN MASTER MUMON[1]

I was facilitating a workshop in Germany when an elegant woman, born in Africa and raised in Switzerland, began to share. She told the group the story of how her family fled to Europe when political instability overtook her country. She was only six years old when they left everything, braving their way north as homeless refugees. She had retained nothing from her early life, not even a memory. Everything was stripped. She started her life over in a completely strange land.

As a young girl, she was aware that she was different from the Swiss; her language, her style of dress, and the color of her skin set her apart. She sensed instinctively her differences were dangerous, and without being told, she strove to fit in. She felt especially vulnerable when other Africans drew attention to themselves or behaved in ways that were not acceptable in Swiss culture.

She wished they understood, like she did, that it was their obligation to blend in. She worked hard at finding her place in a foreign culture. Most importantly, she learned to dwell in what she called "the Universal," that aspect of human experience beyond differences: beyond skin color, nationality, and social status; beyond relative conditions altogether. Her recognition of this True Nature was obvious. She was a stunning presence and poignant beyond her words. Everyone in the room felt moved as she spoke.

Our true home is our spiritual nature, a place of safety and ultimate equality. From this original source, we have so much in common. We are all born into a great mystery. We breathe the same air, feel the warmth of the same sun on our skin, and look up at the same moon and stars at night. We strive to be happy in our own misguided ways, and we all experience challenge, suffering, and moments of despair. It has been said that "the tears of the red, yellow, black, brown, and white man are all the same."[2] And in time, we will all die.

As humans, we may reside deeply together in being, but we are also exceptional in our ability to actively cooperate. The famous sociobiologist and Harvard professor E. O. Wilson says that we are one of the most convivial species on the planet, along with ants, termites, and bees.[3] We have built megacities where ten, fifteen, or twenty million people live together. This is astounding. These are our own massive hills and hives, and we go about our business with every bit the same determination and cooperation as these insects do. With this extraordinary ability to live and work together, we thrive as a species.

Another profound commonality that we share is family and culture. Families provide a haven of intimacy and protection (as well as pain and neurosis). Their shared history, values, and activity are woven tightly together with their DNA. Culture creates another tight boundary of sameness around us. We associate with the people who look like us, talk like us, dress the same, and share our worldview. The sameness feels good and safe. We can relax with people like us and nod our head in agreement, erasing any lines between us. We relish harmony like this in our social circles. It feels good to be reflected by people who look like us, who think like us, who do the same things we do. We are stronger because we are the same. They say that in our evolutionary past, difference often equaled threat, but our tightly knit togetherness ensured safety and survival.

DIFFERENCE

In the German workshop, we had been exploring these forms of commonality through meditation, listening, and open communication practice. Then we switched to talking about our differences, braving a conversation about the refugee crisis in Europe. It was this conversation that prompted the woman from Switzerland to speak.

After telling us about her family's journey and the tremendous efforts she made to blend in, she went on to say that this conversation was the first time in her life she had spoken about her differences out loud: the challenges of being African in Europe, of being black where most people are white, and of having little money in a country with enormous wealth. It was a mind-stopping moment and hard to accept that she would feel so limited to speak up in a European democratic culture.

Her silence was probably not due to her differences, but the value judgments that are placed on them. It isn't simply that our skin is black or white; it is that one is considered better than the other. With the value difference of better and worse comes an array of disadvantages. Those disadvantages lead to injustice; that injustice hardens into oppression. There comes a point when we can no longer simply talk about our differences. We have to talk about our judgments, our emotional distress, our shared history of pain and oppression. A conversation that includes all of this is immensely challenging. So we avoid these conversations and, like our Swiss friend, just try to get along.

When the workshop was over, the memorable woman came up to me, squeezed my hand, and with deep sincerity in her eyes, thanked me for giving her the opportunity to speak. She said she felt an entirely new sensation in her body. She felt integrated and joyful in a way she had never experienced.

I didn't feel that she should thank me. I confessed to her that I struggle in my own way to learn to have real conversations about my differences with the people I live and work with. But I want to learn how to do it because I sense that I cannot be whole without including them; nor will I be complete without their taking me in. I know that only together can we address the cruelty and injustice in the world. So I ventured tentatively into talking about difference, and she helped me understand more than I did before our conversation. I believe that our capacity to acknowledge difference, to be willing to explore it, and to include diversity of opinions and styles within our relationships and communities is a sign of health and vitality.

SAME AND DIFFERENT

Ultimately, as they say in Zen, "Everything [is] the same; everything [is] distinct."[4] When it comes to humans, we are both alike and different. One day, when my son Willie and I were in New York City together on the subway, he looked around and said to me, "Everyone is different, and everyone looks just like their own parents."

Indeed, Willie is like me. He has my dark eyebrows, strong opinions, and sensitivity to the feelings of others. Then again, he is not like me. He has Down syndrome. He has one more chromosome than I do, and that tiny speck of a difference shows up in everything he does.

On the day he was born, I looked at the midwife, who had a concerned look on her face, and asked, "Is everything OK?"

She responded, "I am worried about how he looks."

I gazed into his tiny new face, saw the unusual fold in his eyes, and said aloud, "He has Down syndrome." Then I sank into a stunned abyss, a dark hole that felt infinite and eternal. I thought I would never return, that I would always be in this terrible difference that separated me from the simple joy that a new mother usually feels.

But in the few days after Willie's birth, I realized that in spite of the grief I felt, I was still the same as other new mothers. My daily routines of feeding, changing diapers, and delighting in his new life captured my attention and offered me the sweet pleasure of attending to a newborn. I found refuge in all the ways I was the same as every other mother, from getting up to feed the baby when I was exhausted to enjoying the quietude of holding a baby in my arms and settling down at night. I soon realized that all mothers endure pain and fear for their child's future; I was not alone in that. Like them, I had hopes for my baby, and I knew there would be difficulties ahead.

Later on, my recognition of this profound sameness carried me through the times when Willie's differences did become difficult. Sometimes I struggled at school, sometimes in an encounter with a stranger, or sometimes with my own family because I was the only one who had a child with a disability and I felt the isolation of that. But Willie's unique perspective, his simple language, and way of expressing himself have been consistently enriching. And the immediacy of his affection and his sweetness is sometimes so pure as to be overwhelming. I am so profoundly touched by him—in the ways we are the same and the ways that we are different.

THE PRACTICE

1. Pick someone in your life whom you are close to.
2. Make a short list of the ways you are the same.
3. Now reflect on several of your differences. Which differences give you pleasure and are easy to include in your relationship?
4. What are the differences between you that are difficult to work with?

TOGETHER, THEN APART

The truth is, we're better off apart,
It just kills me to admit it.

—ANONYMOUS

I remember distinctly when I was about twelve, my best girlfriend—the one with whom I had spent every spare moment since I was about eight—and I started to disagree. Before that, we had worn the same kind of shoes, donned the same haircut, and outfitted ourselves in the same pleated skirts and navy blue windbreakers. We were all about our identification with each other. For us, seeming to be the same person was far more compelling than our distinctiveness.

Suddenly, right before we went into junior high school, our love of sameness began to change, and we started to quarrel about what we liked and didn't like.

Where we used to go together shopping, looking at clothes we couldn't afford to buy and admiring them anyway, cooing like two doves over shapes and material, now each time one of us made a bid for agreement, the other hemmed, hawed, shrugged, and walked away.

An unexpected rift grew between us, soon it was a chasm, and before long we were living in entirely separate worlds. I didn't have even a hint at the time that this eruption of difference could be seen as healthy differentiation.[1] All I knew was that our stream of togetherness had become rocky, and unable to clear the differences away, we drifted miles apart.

Studies in human development reveal that our focus on our similarities or differences changes throughout the course of our lives.[2] In other words, we are caught in the tension between the relaxation of the status quo and the exciting encounter with difference. This contrast is a constant on the path toward greater awareness and growth.

A baby is swaddled in sameness with mommy, while a two-year-old shouts out his differences with an emphatic "No!" or "Mine," shaking his formidable toddler head.[3] An adolescent's developmental task is similar, although a little more complicated. A healthy teenager moves from safe identification with parents and family, shifting his or her desire for sameness to his or her set of peers. The teenager feels strength and autonomy when butting heads over differences with the mother, but feels threatened and alone when he or she falls out with a friend on Facebook.

Belonging to one's group of friends is so important, but when they reject the teen, the family provides a warm blanket of togetherness again, comforting him or her in her moment of difference. These coming and goings are painful for teenagers, especially girls, but when a teen is supported properly by his or her family in the right amount, they help the teen to begin to integrate the warmth of communion and the chilly, but excellent, freedom of autonomy.

For some of us, as soon as we reach adulthood, our need for belonging and sameness becomes the predominant value. After exploring differences as an adolescent, we choose to settle in with our kind of people—securing family relationships, finding a steady group of friends who share our style and values, and making very few changes to our group, our church, or our worldview after we leave home.

In these contexts, we work to keep differences down because they cause anxiety, especially within our close, protected circle. So we practice getting along, learning to accommodate, adapt, and participate in established social norms. We don't "rock the boat"; we "let sleeping dogs lie" and refuse to "stir the pot." True, we don't express our private opinions frequently, because harmony is our most important value.

There comes a time, however, when the rocky road of differentiation may beckon again. Something in us wants to grow and change. For example, we may discover that our sexual orientation is forbidden in the religion we grew up in, but we can no longer remain in denial about it. So we are forced to move on. Sometimes we leave with resentment, sometimes relief, or most often with a combination of both. If we suffer an accident or loss like a permanent injury after years of competitive sports, we may lose our friends who are athletes while we try to heal our body and reorganize our life purpose. Some of us find ourselves differentiating from old friends when a suitable marriage partner doesn't appear in the script or we don't have children when everyone else does. Things change, differences accrue, life moves on. And we move with it.

I have heard of soldiers who left the military when making war lost its meaning for them, or business execs who quit working when making money lost its shine. It is not uncommon for a member of a close-knit spiritual community to end up at odds with the teacher. Or for a college student to sometimes have a falling out with a valued mentor. An unexpected exile like this can be incredibly disorientating and depressing, and for some people, it constitutes a dark night of the soul.

But periods of exile propel deep questioning, and it takes courage to move from the security of our sameness into new and different worlds. These are times when we have to go it alone, addressing our deepest question on its own rigorous terms. We may have to ask, "What has real meaning in my life?" Or "Who am I beyond family, community, or a mentor?" Or "What is my unique life purpose?"

This kind of truth seeking and the self-reliance that inevitably comes from it can disrupt the continuity of our life. On the other hand, authentic searching supports our distinctiveness, giving us permission to become truly who we are. We learn to speak our own truth and to stop habitually accommodating, blending in, or, worse, coping with people. As we deeply learn to recognize our differences as a valid part of our life, we will start to grant others theirs.

If we are able to work with the tension of difference, we become confident in our ability to discuss and integrate ways in which we are not the same. Difference is no longer translated as a problem to be rectified or a rejection, as in the moment when my young girlfriend and I turned on our heels, walking away from each other. Rather, it becomes interesting. Suddenly, we want to notice the differences: not to judge them as wrong so quickly, but to name and explore them. We are willing to engage in more difficult communications, exchanging points of view and navigating uneasy feelings. We are willing to take risks and make mistakes. We begin to develop a love for the flavor of difference and its enlivening and disrupting impact. Paradoxically, we are drawn to others who seek the same thing. Pretty soon, we are surrounded in the sameness with people who enjoy differences. Living more deeply within this paradox, we no longer seek exclusive identification with sameness or difference. We are neither a conformist nor a rebel, but appreciate the interplay of both in our lives.

We enjoy the natural boundary around our family, while loving the mix of in-laws at family occasions. We revel in the intensity of a World Cup match or a college football rivalry, but a defeat in the finals doesn't feel like losing to a conquering army. (Well, maybe it does, but not for as long). We may be perfectly happy to stop back into the church of our childhood, feeling at home in the prayers, hymns, and liturgy, but notice that we are free from exclusive identification with one religion. We are happy to belong, but we love the freedom and autonomy of being alone. We discover that our deepest nature is the unity that includes diversity.

There comes a time when we have delved into differences so deeply that our attitude toward them changes. We have to go further than just recognizing our differences; we have to negotiate them, make compromises and agreements regarding them, but it is helpful to recognize first that they are legitimate and not wrong. Eventually, our attitude changes toward our conflicts when they come up. We begin to see conflicts as an exaggerated difference. They don't have to result in ongoing quarrels or estrangements. We may still feel threatened in moments—that never seems to go away—but we have the courage to work with them directly, trusting the innate intelligence of the struggle.

It is a very freeing experience to suddenly realize that differences between us are not only OK—they are stimulating and worthwhile. This realization heightens our confidence to bring them out directly and openly. Once we do, we can learn how to navigate them more efficiently. There is less dread, less shame, and less blame. Instead of taking hours and days to talk something over, we can take only minutes to work out a snag because we have already created the grooves in our consciousness that accommodate difference. We aren't as threatened. Our body is not so reactive. So conversation is interesting and resolving problems is more efficient. The next question becomes how we can bring this kind of light heart and light foot into our social action in the world. This is a question worth living. Finding this kind of ease in our personal lives is the first step.

THE PRACTICE

1. Remember a time when you were close to someone and then it changed.
2. Try to recall what happened.
3. How did you experience the loss?
4. Did you ever come back together again?

THE EGO DIVIDES

When the awakened state of mind is crowded by ego, it takes on the character of an underlying instinct.

—CHÖGYAM TRUNGPA[1]

I have a funny postcard on my fridge. It is of a lovely girl kneeling in a garden. She looks charming with her hair swept back into a neat ponytail and her cheerful cardigan sweater with pearl buttons and a pink-and-white skirt draped over her knees. She is holding a small spade in her hand, seemingly happy and fulfilled in her world. The caption reads, *Gardening, yoga, bubble baths, meditation, and I still want to smack somebody.*

No kidding. After lots of yoga, meditation, and a few bubble baths myself, I sometimes feel the same. I have done years and years of practice—meditating, listening, questioning, using all the skills that I am writing about—and all of a sudden, I can feel completely threatened and overwhelmed. I have come to see that there is some serious ancient hardwiring in my brain and nervous system that, even after years of meditation, is all fight or flight.

We are groomed by evolution to focus on protecting ourselves whenever we sense a threat to our well-being. In our modern context, we may not be physically threatened. But in our highly social and emotionally complex world, threats to our ego or self-concept can feel every bit as perilous. Our strategies for self-protection range from avoidance to fighting to sarcastic humor to drug addiction.

On the surface, our habit of protecting ourselves looks perfectly appropriate. But deep down—if we are honest—we can see that we are responding to adult challenges exactly like we learned to do as a child. We deal with our differences just like our parents did: we withdraw our love; we express ourselves passive-aggressively (like being late for dinner or forgetting to do the favor we promised). Or we flutter about, smoothing things over like a harried housewife straightening up before the guests arrive. Or we might be chronically irritable and critical, like our friend in the postcard whose anxiety is translated immediately into aggression. Whatever our tendency, these are deeply held patterns that limit our capacity to simply observe or stay present, let alone react in a new way.

These habits are examples of being "mindless." Mindlessness is described by researchers as "a state of rigidity in which one adheres to a single perspective and acts automatically."[2] They say that in the mindless state, fresh outcomes are virtually impossible because our responses are so automatic. So how do we go about cultivating greater openness and flexibility in the face of intense feelings of threat? Easier said than done. Threat is real.

AMYGDALA HIJACK

It helps to understand how the brain and nervous system work when we experience threat. Our brains contain two tiny regions called amygdala, one on each side, behind the eyes and the optical nerves. These amygdala have been called the brain's "smoke detector."[3] They are responsible for detecting fear and preparing our body for an emergency response.

When the brain perceives a threat, the amygdala sounds an alarm, releasing a cascade of chemicals in the body. Stress hormones, such as adrenaline and cortisol, flood our system, immediately preparing us for fight or flight. When this deeply instinctive function takes over, it is called "amygdala hijack."[4] In common psychological parlance we say, "We've been triggered." We feel immediate changes such as an increased heart rate or sweaty palms. Our breathing becomes more shallow and rapid as we take in more oxygen, preparing to bolt if we have to. Other sensations occur, such as a quivering in our solar plexus, limbs, or our voice. We may notice heat flushing our face, our throat constricting, or the back of our neck or jaw tightening. Our shoulders contract like a cat hunching up to protect its tender and vulnerable underside. Our breathing changes suddenly, becoming more shallow and rapid. Like any creature in the wild, we are in the grip of a highly efficient but prehistoric set of physiological responses. Above all, our body is prepared to do what it takes to protect ourselves. If there is one thing that creates an intense feeling of separation from others, it is the fight-or-flight response.

By the way, these sensations are not exactly pleasant; they are not meant for relaxation. They are designed to move us to action. It reminds me of what it is like to listen to a crying baby on an airplane. It can be intensely uncomfortable. The sound of a wailing baby creates an impulse in the body to act, to do something for the baby.

To simply sit and listen is difficult, to say the least. The more the baby cries, the more discomfort we feel.

When the amygdala fires, it creates other changes in the brain. It shuts down the pathways to the prefrontal cortex, the center of consciousness where we maintain our intention. So in a heated conversation we may lose our sense of purpose or become disoriented. Our ability to think clearly also vanishes. Complex decision making rapidly disappears, as does our access to multiple perspectives. When our attention narrows like this, we find ourselves trapped in the one perspective that makes us feel the safest: "I'm right and you're wrong." This is true even when normally we can easily include multiple points of view in our awareness. This is why we can sometimes look back at a dysfunctional interaction when we were triggered, asking ourselves, "What exactly happened there? I'm not normally like that."

Under ordinary circumstances, we can easily direct our attention, but in the throes of amygdala hijack, we lose this ability. In addition, our memory becomes untrustworthy. Have you ever been in a fight with your partner or friend, and you literally can't remember a positive thing about them? It is as though the brain drops the memory function altogether in an effort to equip us to survive the threat in this moment and live for another day. When our memory is compromised like this, we can recall almost nothing from our past that might help us calm down. In fact, we can't remember much of anything. Instead, we are filled with the flashing red light of the feelings indicating "Danger—react. Danger—protect. Danger—attack."

All of these changes in the brain result in what we have called a "reactive" or "mindless" state. As soon as we lose access to the prefrontal cortex, we are prevented from choosing how we want to live our life because the old protective mechanism in the nervous system does it for us—even before we glimpse the possibility of a choice.

MINDFULNESS

Bringing our attention to the here and now and closely observing what happens in our own interior is called "mindfulness."[5] Mindfulness is the perfect awareness technique to employ when we feel a threat to our ego—whether at work or home. It allows us to override the conditioned nervous system with conscious awareness. Instead of attacking or recoiling, and later justifying our reactions, we can learn to stay present, participate in regulating our own nervous system, and eventually develop new, freer, and more helpful ways of interacting.

Our analogy to the crying baby on the airplane might be helpful here as we try to imagine how to stay present in these kinds of situations. It is difficult to sit on a plane listening to the distress of a crying infant, feeling the discomfort in our body and mind. But with no other options available except to stay in our seat while the plane gets ready for takeoff, we do manage to sit still. We may divert our attention, focus on a magazine, look out the window, or read an old text message before we turn off the phone, but we don't get up and leave the plane. This is an example of how it is possible to sit still with bodily discomfort. Going one step further, we can become curious about the feelings and impulses in our body as they arise.

There are different approaches to working with a provoked nervous system and intense emotions, but they all have some elements in common. Here are four simple steps, which I also describe in my book *Everything Is Workable*.[6] I try to use these steps when I find myself with an overloaded nervous system and a body racing with a fight-or-flight impulse.

Step 1: Stay Present

The first step in practicing mindfulness when we're triggered is to notice we're provoked. We may notice a change in our tone of voice, gripping sensations in the belly, or a sudden desire to withdraw. Each of us has particular bodily and behavioral cues that alert us to the reality that we feel threatened and are therefore running on automatic pilot.

We have to decide to stay put and present, to be curious and explore our experience. For me, it helps to remind myself to relax. I use a visual cue that involves my son. When I'm worked up, he has the habit of looking at me, raising and lowering his hands in a calming fashion and saying, "Easy, Windmill." I try to reflect on this, and it helps me calm down because he's so charming when he does it.

Step 2: Let Go of the Story

This might be the most difficult part of the practice. We need to completely let go of the thinking and judging mind. This is a very challenging step because when we feel threatened, the mind immediately fills with all kinds of difficult thoughts and stories about what's happening. But we must be willing to forget the story, just for a minute, because there is a feedback loop between our thoughts and our body. If the negative thoughts persist, so do the stressful hormones. It isn't that we're wrong, but we will be clearer in our perceptions when the nervous system has relaxed.

Step 3: Focus on the Body

Now simply focus on feeling and exploring whatever sensations arise in the body. Feel them naturally, just as they are, not trying to control or change them. Allow the mind to be as open as possible, noticing the different places in the body where sensations occur: what is tight, shaky, rushing, or hurts. Pay attention to the different qualities and textures of the sensations, and the way things change and shift. We can also notice how biased we are against unpleasant or more intense sensations.

Step 4: Finally, Breathe

Everybody knows that it helps to breathe. There are many different qualities of the breath, but we only need to learn about two: rhythm and smoothness.[7] If we focus on these two dimensions, even for a few short minutes, the production of the cortisol and adrenaline will stop.

To breath rhythmically means that the in-breath and out-breath occur repeatedly at the same intervals. So if we inhale, counting 1, 2, 3, 4, and then exhale, counting

1, 2, 3, 4, 5, 6; then inhale again, counting 1, 2, 3, 4, and then exhale again, counting 1, 2, 3, 4, 5, 6—this establishes rhythm.

At the same time, we should invite the breath to be even or smooth, meaning that the volume of the breath stays consistent as it moves in and out, like sipping liquid through a narrow straw. If we manage those two qualities for just a few minutes, the breath assists us in remaining present, making it possible to stay with intense sensation in the body.

Paying attention to our body reestablishes equilibrium faster, restoring our ability to think, to listen, and to relate. This takes practice, but eventually we retrain ourselves to respond rather than to react. We learn the art of transmuting emotion so that our anger becomes clarity and resolve; our sadness opens us to compassion, while jealousy becomes fuel for change.

There will also be certain moments when we fail. But each time we succeed in being mindful of our body in moments of distress, we develop our capacity. Even more, we may observe something new when we're mindful: a moment of pause, an unexpected question that arises, or a laugh that erupts. When anything new happens, taking note of it helps to free us of the pattern to our old way of doing things. Before we know it, our old habit of fight or flight is changing, and the world is a safer place.

THE PRACTICE

To recap four simple steps:

1. Take the opportunity to become intimate with the feelings of a provoked nervous system. The next time you feel triggered, simply intend to stay present—for two minutes, five minutes, or ten minutes.

2. Be sure to watch the story that you are telling yourself about the situation, and to the extent possible, let it go and go back to noticing feeling instead.

3. Notice precisely what is occurring. Where is the sensation? What is it like? Note the texture, tone, and temperature of sensations, including changes, shifts, or surges. Notice the tendency to move away from what feels unpleasant.

4. Practice breathing rhythmically and smoothly, just to get the hang of it. Notice how working with the breath softens the intensity of sensation.

4
___

MINDFULNESS AND MEDITATION

Mindfulness isn't difficult, we just need to remember to do it.

—SHARON SALZBERG[1]

Willie is a creature of habit. One of his routines is to spend part of the weekend with his best lifelong friend, Isaac, who also has Down syndrome. Their Friday night ritual is to eat takeout and watch reruns of *Saturday Night Live*. On Saturday around noon, I usually bring them sandwiches for lunch.

When I arrive, Isaac goes downstairs to fetch a soda to share from the pantry. While I unpack lunch at the kitchen counter, he brings two glasses from the cupboard, filling each half full with ice from the freezer. Then he sets the glasses down right next to each other and places the can of soda next to the glass. Then he pauses. His demeanor behind the counter is like a science teacher in a lab coat and black glasses who is about to demonstrate an experiment showing how static electricity works or what happens when you put magnesium into dry ice. His glasses are ready; his ice cubes are in place. Slowly he pries the can open.

Carefully, he lifts the can and begins to pour the first glass. A fizzy stream of dark liquid drizzles down into the glass, hissing and foaming. When there is an inch of liquid in the glass, he slows down to a trickle and then stops pouring. Now he deliberately moves the can over to the second glass. He begins to pour again, filling the second glass to precisely the same level as the first, letting it froth and sizzle. This back-and-forth process goes on for five minutes until both glasses are filled to the top. Then he sets the empty can to rest and stands quietly in front of his work. It is complete. He and the can are both empty.

Isaac's drink pouring is a pristine example of mindfulness. He is deliberate and focused, yet relaxed. He is aware of his intention and each movement, connecting fully with his environment through his eyes and hands, moving fluidly through to his goal. Most importantly, he is deeply concentrated in the here and now, and he is free of judgments about himself as good or bad, right or wrong, as he attends to his task. Mindfulness is just that—bringing fluid and focused attention to our activity here and now, while remaining free of the stream of discursive comments and judgments that so often distort our experience of the moment.

There is mounting scientific research on the positive effects of mindfulness.[2] According to this research, the practice of mindfulness improves our concentration and enables us to be more open and mentally flexible. We learn to stay present to difficult emotions and feeling states, and over time, having cultivated nonjudgmental awareness, we can simply observe our interior landscape without incessant self-criticism. We develop the ability to view things and situations in our ordinary life with a similar kind of nonjudgmental, open attention.

Eventually, that openness extends to how we view other people. We see others for who they are simply and directly without the need to make them good or bad, right or wrong. In this way, we become more patient, nonjudgmental, and tolerant of the differences we have with others. Mindfulness ripens into heartfulness, awareness gives rise to compassion, and curiosity overcomes fear. Eventually, we become more at home in the world, more trusting, and we want to offer something worthwhile to our existence, to participate in creating beauty in our life and that of others.

MINDFULNESS IN THE WORLD

In 1979, Jon Kabat-Zinn[3] brought mindfulness meditation to the medical world in the treatment of the chronically ill. His work sparked the use of mindfulness for the treatment of a variety of conditions, mainly chronic pain, and the practice seems to have spread like wildfire. Mindfulness is being taught now everywhere—from therapy offices to schools to prisons to corporate settings. Google is probably the best-known company offering mindfulness training to its employees.

As a practice for communication or conflict resolution skills, mindfulness is newer still,[4] but the practice has every bit as powerful an impact as it does on pain. Becoming mindful and attentive when a difference arises is foundational to helping us to see our entrenched habitual patterns and, eventually, helping us develop new ways to interact.

Threat provokes such intense sensations in our body and mind that sitting still seems wildly counterintuitive and impossible. But the first step is to learn to sit still and simply pay attention. It is challenging to observe our experience and become familiar with our patterns of reacting. If we want to change, we have to begin by studying what happens to us in stressful situations. We must become really curious about what is going on inside of us when we feel threatened. This involves stilling ourselves enough to watch our thoughts and to feel our emotional states directly—not an easy thing to do. A sitting meditation practice reinforces our ability to remain present but detached.

Mindfulness involves asking questions of ourselves like: How does my body feel right now? What sensations are rushing through me? Is there a buildup of heat, a nervous flurry, or a surge of nausea? Where is the sensation? In my solar plexus, my stomach, or my throat?

What kinds of urges am I experiencing? An impulse to get in the car and run an errand? Or do I feel like falling asleep on the couch, going to the fridge, or pouring myself a drink? Do I want to quickly pick up the phone and tell someone about my situation? Or am I going to get busy and go back to work?

Of our emotional state, we can ask, What feelings are pervading my nervous system? Where do I feel them? Can I locate one feeling or several different ones as they swirl and shift in my system? Can I name and distinguish them (e.g., shame, hatred, embarrassment), or are they arising as one overwhelming whole? How quickly do these feelings change and shift? What feelings do I have toward the other person, and how do my feeling states combine to affect my thinking?

Then we can bring our attention to our mind. What thoughts come up when my system is agitated? What is their tone? Are they measured and reasonable, or are they filled with blame, accusations, or justifications? What do I think should happen next? Can I remain aware with my sensations, feelings, and thoughts, or is my mind rushing mindlessly to replay the past or strategize a response in the future?

What story do I tell myself about my role in the conflict? Is it a familiar story, one that I have told many times before? Is the other person to blame, and am I, coincidentally, right again?

Can we remain aware and curious about the totality of our sensations, feelings, and thoughts? Is it possible to engage our open, unconditioned awareness and simply experience what is happening without judging it as good or bad, right or wrong?

It takes a lot of practice, but by repeatedly bringing mindful attention and the broad space of awareness to experience, we learn about who we are and what we do. As we begin to substitute our habitual responses with presence and curiosity, we begin to retrain our nervous system.

SITTING MEDITATION

I grew up riding horses in the mountains where I live in Utah. I believe this is how I learned meditation as a young girl. When you a ride horse, your first move is to make gentle contact with the animal. I usually did that first by putting a calm hand on the horse's neck and then stroking and patting his broad body, brushing his beautiful coat, and combing his mane and tail. The smell of a horse is inviting, and so are their large eyes and puffs of breath, meeting me with their nostrils, breathing deeply my scent. It is an exchange.

Then you mount up. Settling into your seat is a lot like sitting on a cushion. You bring full awareness to the place where sits bones, rump, and thighs make contact with the saddle. The seat is everything. Then your spine floats upright and true, erect with relaxed shoulders. The reins rest lightly in your hands, in the same way that we form a mudra in meditation: precise, empty, and, at the same time, full. Both practices involve the subtlety of hands in guiding and stabilizing.

When we make a deep relationship to our own body, open our heart, and quiet our mind, we are in the best position to meet the animal, ourselves, and the world. Becoming one with the horse, our senses open to the world—to the trees, the waters, the sounds and smells of nature. Human, horse, the landscape—just one thing.

Sometimes, when I took a long ride, my mind would be filled with the thoughts of the day. I would be thinking about a gazillion things, some pleasant, some worrisome. And the longer the day wore on, the more the thoughts wore out, till at the end of the day as I came down the canyons and out of the mountains, my mind was as still and empty as a pine tree in the wind. This was riding meditation.

There are different schools of sitting meditation and different techniques for the practice. But in all methods, we practice being mindful and aware. We sit upright: stable, relaxed, and attentive, allowing the breath to come and go, observing the arising of thoughts, feelings, bodily sensations. Like my long days riding a horse when I was young, the mind may be distracted and busy in the beginning, streaming discursive comments and judgments that cloud vision and compromise our direct experience of the moment. But after some time sitting, cultivating calm presence in the here and now, we calm down, settle, and just sit.

Meditation, while subtle, is a powerful practice for waking up to ourselves. We learn how to be present to our immediate experience, without dwelling in the pleasurable details or avoiding the more painful ones. The more we sit still, cultivating this unbiased, flowing awareness, the more the body becomes stable and the mind becomes calm and clear. Our awareness becomes less distorted and less judgmental. Our sense perceptions are clearer. Colors are brighter, sounds more distinct; the environment is alive and very real. You can say that we dissolve divisions in the mind to become "one with" or the "same as" our experience. As we have already talked about, sameness equals peace.

Meditation is a most worthy discipline and extremely helpful in our effort to become more aware of who we truly are. In turn, it helps in our relationship with others. Our mind becomes suppler, a little less fixed on hard lines of black and white. Our heart is more open and compassionate toward others. This strengthens our goodwill and supports us in acting in ways that others can respect. When we do get upset or thrown off-balance, like when a horse ditches quickly to avoid a fright, we are much quicker to regain our composure and find our seat amid all of life's inevitable ups and downs. Just like exercise, there is an enormous range in commitment to meditation, from full-time meditators who live in monasteries to those who sit still for a few minutes each day riding the bus to work. But if there is one basic practice that will help us be present to ourselves and, therefore, capable of being present to others, sitting meditation is it.

THE PRACTICE

1. The next time you find yourself in a conflict or negative emotional state, give all of your attention to your immediate experience.
2. Begin with the body, noticing what sensations you can identify. Where are they located? What is their texture and tone? How are they changing?
3. What feelings can you name? Where are they located, and how are they shifting and changing? If you could speak about them, what would you say?
4. Finally, notice your thoughts. What story are you telling yourself about the situation? Can you suspend the story for now?
5. Now feel the surge of energy that courses through your body, including anything chaotic and unpleasant.

6. Practice allowing the sensations, feelings, and thoughts to come and go without manipulating them. Create an open space of unbiased awareness in which the entire play of experience is simply observed and noted. Commit to allowing things to be just as they are until tomorrow, and then think about whether to take any action.

LISTENING

The Supreme Skill

Listening is an act of surrender.

—BRIAN ENO[1]

Listening is the powerful, soothing agent of all communication. Listening is the best tool there is to lower anxiety, diminish division, and open into sameness, into togetherness. Listening will help almost anyone who is triggered to calm down. The deeply beautiful and profound thirteenth-century Persian poet Rumi says, "Beyond ideas of wrongdoing and right doing, there is a field. I'll meet you there."[2] Listening is a gateway into that open field.

Nobody listens well without first deciding to. At least, I never do. When I do decide to listen, I make a choice to put my own thoughts and perceptions on pause, empty out, and open up my senses to take in the other person. I cross over, if only for a few minutes, into their world.

I remember the first time I decided to listen to someone who was upset, rather than trying to get them to calm down. I don't remember the exact details of what had happened, just that we were on a camping trip and it was cold. Something had gone wrong, and my friend was pitching a fit, as they say. I recall just how mad she was, the intensity in her face and voice, her dark, pinched eyebrows, her breath puffing outrage mixed with a plea for me to understand why she was so upset.

My first impulse was to tell her it was OK; everything would be all right. Then it occurred to me that she didn't want to hear that. She didn't want to hear anything. She wanted to be heard; otherwise, she probably wouldn't have been shouting. I told myself to relax and see this outburst as just more of the bad weather, and I started listening to what she was saying. I distinctly remember the warm sensation of letting go move through me. Somehow, I managed to drop my wish for things to be different—for the weather to be different, for her to be different. Instead, I went with sameness and found a willingness to listen and to see the world for a moment like she did. She must have felt heard because a tremendous amount of tension dissolved and she started to calm down naturally. It seems obvious now that listening was the better choice, but at the time, my habit was to assure her, to change her, to ask her to be different. I was the one who changed instead. I switched strategy, and for me, more than for her, it was a relief.

LIKE MEDITATION

Listening has a lot in common with meditation. Both involve a clear intention of bringing attention to this moment, opening up, and letting go of the preoccupations of the self. This means that we suspend our internal thoughts and quiet the viewpoints most closely held as "mine." We just let them go, turning off our opinions like shutting off our cell phone.

As easy as that sounds, it is more difficult to do than giving in to our viewpoints. Those silent opinions give us a reference point to hold on to. It is like having an internal handrail in the mind. I can listen to you as long as I have a sense of solidity, of safety, of security inside myself. If I give up the attachment to what I think and feel, I'm afraid I'll drop into a kind of free fall. I'll lose my grip on things. I won't really know who I am or where I am going. Who knows, I might even die. I know this sounds dramatic and silly, but at some level, this is how tightly we hold on to our own perspective.

Listening and meditating involve letting go—releasing our tight grip on things in the mind. We become familiar with the sensation of release. At first it feels like falling, but once we have befriended it, once we have learned to relax with it, it feels good to let go. Letting go is another form of sameness. Our private opinions and judgments no longer create a division between us and the person speaking. We simply join with their experience. We become one and the same.

MORE PERSPECTIVES

Listening is an avenue to a greater world. It is an opening into a way of seeing, of feeling, of knowing that is beyond our own. When I listen to a child, I hear the sweet perceptions of a child. When I listen to an old person, I feel the creakiness moving into my own bones. When I have a good teacher and bend my ear toward them, they speak to me of possibilities that I may never have imagined. Listening is our ticket to a greater reality, one with broad vistas and a wide-open sky.

Before we can improve our listening skills, there is a question worth asking ourselves: Are we ready for a different set of perceptions, a different way of seeing things? Most of the people I know would say we are, and yet, we often behave as if there is only one correct perspective—and it just happens to be *mine*.

Listening to another perspective doesn't necessarily mean we agree with it. We sometimes fear that if we take in another point of view, it will be mistaken for concession. But if we are clear in our own mind that listening doesn't mean agreement, we can open with confidence to other points of view. We can practice just listening with an open, curious, and not-knowing mind. We literally join with the perceptions of the other and become the same with them. Usually, when we listen, we still have boundaries in our mind. We want to share our experience, we are waiting to give advice, or we are holding a set of quiet opinions. Open listening is free from the usual barrage of unnecessary judgments and disapprovals that create divisions in our open field of sameness.

I recently had an occasion to practice my listening skills. My husband and I had been having a conversation about our daughter's pet dog. We both like the dog, but we disagree about whether we want to take care of her. I don't want to because she has an unsociable habit of peeing on the carpet, scratching doors, and doing other damage in the house. She's not a bad girl, but she is anxious and old. It is stressful to have to keep a close eye on her.

I went out of town for a week, and when I came home, my husband was taking care of her again. I was fairly sure we had both decided we wouldn't babysit the dog anymore. But I saw I was wrong about that. Once I got over being annoyed, I asked him again why he wanted to take care of the little dog. I felt that I must have missed something the first time around.

I took a breath while he explained that he enjoys taking care of her. He conceded that the dog can be difficult, but he said that he still finds her charming in spite of her habits. He likes her furry little body and her strange shih tzu grimace when she wags her tail. "Also," he added, "it is a way for me to express support for our daughter while she is in school, and she's so busy." He said he wants her to know that, in a bind, he doesn't mind stepping in and doing some dog sitting.

I tried to listen. I finally quieted down my internal protests and listened to what he had to say. I heard him describe his care and felt the sweetness in his voice. I also felt his generosity. Apart from whether we took care of the dog or not, I found that in just letting in his perspective, I really appreciated hearing him express his love.

Listening is an act of emptying out and receiving. Although it is a surrender, it isn't a defeat. It is simply letting go and for a moment becoming one with another point of view. When we listen, sometimes we can ask clarifying questions; sometimes we reflect back what we have heard. (For a full discussion of listening skills, see *Everything Is Workable*.) Most important, we offer the speaker the experience of being heard. Maybe we even extend a little appreciation his or her way for sharing another viewpoint, because if you think about it, no one is required to give their viewpoint, and it's even possible to take that kind of sharing as a form of generosity.

RESISTANCE TO LISTENING

If listening is such an important skill, why don't we do it better than we do? Mostly, we don't do it for all kinds of good reasons. We don't because we are in a hurry. We don't because we think we have heard it all before. We don't because we are busy with e-mails to read, phone calls to return, appointments to get to. Another reason we don't want to listen is because we have judgments about what is being said. We think the person is wrong or that his or her perception is distorted. Maybe we think the person's viewpoint isn't serving him or her well. Whatever it is, our judgments create barriers between us. These become little fences of difference that make the open field of genuine listening much harder to enter.

Finally, a significant reason that we don't listen is that we don't want to feel the pain and discomfort of other people. When someone tells me a distressing story, the first thing I want to do is comfort that person. I believe that I want to ease his or her suffering, but if I look closely, I can see that what I really want is to relieve mine. Because if I join with the pain, it hurts. One time after my father died, I sat having dinner with my mother, who was bewildered and very sad. I tried to say reassuring things to her like an older daughter would. Willie just sat quietly listening to her. Finally, he looked at her in her grief and bewilderment and said simply, "It really hurts."

My mother looked into his eyes and nodded her head very slowly. I could see she felt completely met. She didn't want my advice, but she did want contact. She wanted to feel sad that her husband was gone and to sense someone joining her in that feeling. I thought I was trying to be helpful, but I think I was scared for her and was trying to soothe her grief to quell my own discomfort. But Willie was present; he listened to her and then simply reflected what he had heard.

When friends are going through a rough time, it is helpful to remind ourselves to listen—not to give advice, to attempt to fix the problem, or try to make them feel better. We have a habit of giving people advice, but how often do they really want it? Almost never. But everyone responds well when we are present, receptive, and curious about their experience. Asking real and simple questions is always worthwhile when the questions are genuine.

Finally, I have the most difficulty of all in listening when I am criticized. When someone says something to me that I don't want to hear, I struggle every time—and I mean *every* time. My defenses erupt, and my ego seeks protection even before my conscious mind has registered that I feel threatened. This is true even when I have asked for feedback. So I practice again and again and again, reminding myself to relax when someone is offering me any kind of constructive criticism or negative feedback.

Listening is truly the most effective communication skill there is. Every time there is agitation in a conversation, listening helps to smooth things out. It eases tension and brings the dynamics of speaking and listening into equilibrium. We can use it to calm any situation. Listening is an act of surrender, of becoming one and the same. Like meditation, it involves letting go.

THE PRACTICE

1. Think about the last time someone really listened to you.
2. Reflect on what it was like to have someone else drop his or her opinions and simply open to you and your perspective.
3. What did you experience in your body? Can you recall sensations of relief, of relaxation, of safety setting in?
4. Now think about a person in your life who could use being listened to.
5. Are you willing to give the person a gift of presence and your undivided attention?

EXPRESSING OUR UNIQUENESS

Always be yourself, express yourself.
Have faith in yourself.

—BRUCE LEE[1]

If listening opens up the wide territory of sameness, expressing difference catalyzes conversations. Listening soothes and harmonizes; self-expression stimulates and energizes. Our differences distinguish us from everything else, giving shape to our uniqueness and setting us apart. They remind us that nowhere else in the entire universe is there anything like us—never has been and never will be. We are specific, detailed, and wondrous, made of amazing particularities like our unique face, voice, and fingerprints. Our internal lives are completely our own—our thoughts, feelings, our strange and unusual dreams. Our pain is our own to feel and transform, and if we don't, no one can do it for us.

Each of us has a family history and cultural context with immense similarities to others who belong to our family or culture, but how we experience them differs remarkably. No two siblings remember the family history in quite the same way or tell the same story about the past. The occasion of our birth is unique, and our death is touching in how specific it is among deaths. Everything in between details a distinct path and a distinct story, one worth telling.

We are right to want to tell our story, to give our perspective. Our uniqueness wants and deserves to be fully expressed. The iconic twentieth-century dancer and choreographer Martha Graham has been quoted as saying, "There is a vitality, a life force, an energy, a quickening that is translated through you into action, and there is only one of you in all time, this expression is unique. And if you block it, it will never exist through any other medium and be lost."[2]

Indeed, our perspective is unique because in the whole universe, we are the only one standing right where we are, when we are, looking through our particular lens and seeing what we see. Since we alone inhabit this exact point of view, only we can express it. There is an innate dignity to our viewpoint. Because it is rare, it is intrinsically valuable. Acknowledging this brings us a moment of awe, instilling a profound respect for ourselves and conversely for others. It is difficult to express ourselves when the ego is threatened, but when we relax, our uniqueness is free to shine through.

SELF-EXPRESSION

Uniqueness comes loaded for expression. We say in Zen, "The willow is green; the flowers are red."[3] The plants convey themselves completely. Like them, we don't have to practice expressing ourselves; it is built in. Even our silence shouts who we are. If we are the type to disappear in a crowd, that invisibility communicates something. True, some people are masters at getting attention for their own self-expression through a zany style of dress or an outlandish approach to life, but take a second glance at anybody, and we are all, even those of us who disappear into a crowd, intrinsically, remarkably unique.

To become skilled at honest, open verbal expression, at dropping our defensiveness, and at sharing our unique perspective requires tremendous practice. Including differences in conversation, allowing them to energize and provoke us, but not to alienate us, requires a lot of skill. There are tried and true methods for developing an ability to speak truthfully and from the heart.[4] No matter what method you use, it takes intention and practice.

First, and maybe most importantly, we have to want to. Second, it helps to have someone who wants to listen. The more we have listened to ourselves and connected to our message, the more likely it is that others will listen to us. We must ask ourselves:

What is true for me right now?
What do I really think about this?
How do I really feel?
Am I willing to take the risk of setting myself apart, if just for a few moments?

The next step is that we have to be brave and do it.

"I" STATEMENTS

In any communications skills training, we are immediately advised to use "I" statements. "I" statements are like magic. By beginning a sentence with "I," that simple stroke of a pronoun, we draw a line between ourselves and other people's opinions. This boundary has the potential to energize relationship, as long as it doesn't become defensive.

The first-person perspective is the most intimate and familiar one we have. Using "I" locates our unique point of view inside of our direct experience, freeing everyone else from the need to agree or disagree. "I" doesn't require evidence like "The truth" does. "I" doesn't imply togetherness or consent like "We" does. It simply says, "This is how I see it." There is freedom in that.

Martin Luther King Jr.'s "I Have a Dream"[5] speech has to be one of the most profound and influential "I" statements in modern times. The great civil rights leader and humanitarian has been praised for everything in this speech—his passion, his timing, his use of repetition, and his brilliant ability to move his audience with his deep, booming voice and vast capacity for truth.

I have always admired his use of the first person in that famous line: "I have a dream." Standing in front of an audience of a quarter million people at the Lincoln Memorial in 1963, he rallied the civil rights movement and confronted the failure of America to fulfill its promise to black people.

He uses the third-person perspective many times when he refers to "America," "to the Negro," and to "the bank of justice" and "the bad check." He shifts to the pronoun "we" when engaging his audience's commitment to ethical activism. "We must not be guilty of wrongful deeds. . . . We must forever conduct our struggle on the high plane of dignity and discipline. . . . We will not be satisfied until justice rolls down like waters and righteousness like a mighty stream."

But then he makes his most remarkable move. I've read he wasn't going to mention his dream until the gospel singer Mahalia Jackson shouted to him, "Tell them about the dream, Martin. Tell them about the dream."[6] At that, he put his prepared speech down and began to speak for himself, beginning his sentences with "I." "I say to you today, my friends, even though we face the difficulties of today and tomorrow, I still have a dream."

When he made the shift to "I," to speaking his truth, his energy moved, and he found his own voice. Apparently, the entire tone of the speech shifted from one that people might not remember, to one everyone remembers. The first-person perspective allowed him access to his moral authority, his passion, and his conviction at a whole other level. He began to stir the heart of the crowd as he described his awesome vision for the future. "I have a dream that my four little children will one day live in a nation where they will not be judged by the color of their skin, but by the content of their character."

His first-person perspective was a great source of freedom, for him and for everyone listening. Because of his use of the "I," no one was required to see what he saw, but everyone wanted to. He didn't tell anyone where to go but gave them the choice to go with him. Even today, that speech continues to carry anyone forward who is earnest in the question of freedom and equality.

And while this speech is a consummate example of public speaking, we can still learn from Dr. King's use of the first person in our own conversations. The freedom of speaking what is simply true in our own experience is remarkably freeing. We aren't burdened by Truth in the big sense of the word and don't have to look for agreement from others. We can be true to our own viewpoint and, because of that, remain humble. It is not the only perspective. It is simply one point of view. There are other lessons we can take from this speech to energize and enliven our communications.

FEELINGS

We can learn from Martin Luther King Jr. how important and persuasive it is to include feeling in our speech. His speech is filled with an array of feelings—

from grave disappointment to righteous anger to moral certitude. He recognizes pain in his speech, fatigue, and struggle. And by the end, he still raises up hope and instills exaltation.

When we talk about speaking from the heart, we mean including our feelings. When the heart is on the line, our expressions are immediate. They are felt by others. Including our feeling states humanizes our communication and creates a feeling bond, bringing empathy, identification, and sameness. Conceding that "I am angry" and taking responsibility for it without blame, or confessing that "I am sad," as difficult as that is to do, creates an emotional connection. We feel very vulnerable in intimate conversations, but including those feelings dissolves defensiveness on both sides. Speaking from the heart is an act of care, so even a criticism or challenge can be placed in our message.

Anytime we express our real thoughts and feelings, it creates more truth and reveals a bigger perspective. And anytime someone else shares their truth with us, we should be grateful that we are given the opportunity to see and feel more than we did before. It is a privilege to feel.

SIMPLICITY AND CLARITY

A final lesson we can take from King's speech is the importance of keeping our messages simple and clear. Public speakers prepare their speeches in order to clarify their thinking and deliver a straightforward message that listeners can receive and remember. Often in conversation, particularly when we are discussing our differences, we don't take time to either prepare or to simplify our message.

I remember teaching a communications skills class one day at a tech company in North Carolina. I have a tendency to become too abstract when I talk, too heady. There was a warehouse worker in the session who, every time I lost him with my barrage of words, just looked at me with a grin on his face and said, "Corn bread. Bring it down. Corn bread."

I'll never forget that guy. He was so funny, so kind and real. He wanted to know what I was talking about, and he wouldn't let me get away with obtuseness. But instead of criticizing me and retreating, he stayed right there with me, urging me to communicate better so that we could succeed in understanding one another.

EXPRESSING WANTS AND NEEDS

It is vitally important that if we have a want or need when expressing our differences, we make a simple request like he did. Recently I facilitated a conversation about race in an online forum. It is always tricky territory to talk about race issues in mixed groups because conversations about race in the United States are often filled with anger, resistance, guilt, and lots of verbal land mines. We were taking a risk in even having our conversation. Nobody had to participate, but we were there, doing our best.

Some people in the group wanted to focus on confronting white privilege, the recognition that whites enjoy numerous advantages unavailable to nonwhites, and that our status as whites blinds us to seeing this very problem.[7] Other people believed we shared a deep understanding of white privilege, and it was time to move on, at least for a time, to explore other important perspectives in the conversation. It was one of those binds that a facilitator finds herself in when people disagree about what they want to talk about.

I could feel the tension in the background as people took turns advocating for their choice. We went back and forth for a while, when a young African American man in our group said a very heartfelt thing: "I just want to be heard." His request was so clear, authentic, and straightforward that it immediately changed the entire atmosphere of the conversation. Suddenly, everyone was willing to listen. His use of the first-person perspective created unexpected intimacy, and his sincere request dissolved barriers.

After a pause, an older man, a white European, responded to him by saying simply, "I do want to hear what you have to say. Please go on." The young black man went on, "We are suffering out here. In spite of gains over the last fifty years, we are still struggling every day. I want you to know that." Suddenly, as he spoke and others listened, expressing and listening became one thing. They were no longer transactional. Each gave rise to the other in a deep, mutual flow. With one true expression, the tense atmosphere of difference was transformed into mutual curiosity and exchange.

OBSTACLES TO CLEAR EXPRESSION

Why isn't it easier to speak simply about our thoughts and feelings? Because, as I said earlier, we are very sensitive to safety in communication. We want to be liked, to be seen as smart or together or politically correct; we want to look like we know what we are talking about. We don't want to be judged, and we don't want to make mistakes. So we often play it safe. We listen passively, and we avoid bringing out a different perspective. Another perspective creates energy, for sure, but it also creates potential conflict. Someone says, "I see it differently," and our ears prick up like a dog who hears the rustling of a cat outside the window.

Differences in conversation are hard to manage. They begin by enlivening, but add just one value judgment to the mix, something like "my view is right and yours is wrong," and the conversation quickly becomes tense or even stressful. If we go one step further, tossing in a dose of anxiety, irritation, or anger at the prospect of difference, we have the basis for conflict. After all, what is conflict if not difference exaggerated by intense negative emotion, blaming, and attacks, and what is violence except the primitive impulse to destroy another perspective or a different way of being?

By practicing listening and expressing our differences, we experience our wholeness. Sometimes it is said in the Zen tradition that practice works on us like polishing a piece of wood brings out its fine grain and unique beauty. It is still wood, but each piece is unique and remarkable in its own expression.

THE PRACTICE

1. Notice the next time you want to express your viewpoint.
2. Ask a potential listener if he or she would be willing to give you two minutes of attention to listening to your perspective.
3. If that person agrees, notice the impact of having your viewpoint valued.
4. Speak freely and learn from listening to yourself as you speak.

DEPTH OF FEELING

*Me: "Willie, do you want to share your feelings
with me?"*
Willie: "I think I am fine, and you are, too."

My mother was a powerful feeler. I remember sitting with her one afternoon while she looked at an old photograph of her father. She talked about him for an hour. She must have moved through six or seven distinct emotional states as she gazed at his face. She expressed tenderness, poignancy, intrigue, impatience, anger, remorse, and love. I wondered which of them was most true. I concluded in my young mind that all of her feelings together meant she loved him.

I was about thirteen at the time, and I remember being impressed with her emotional range. It was the first time I remember admiring this particular quality in her unique character. I felt the depth of presence in my mother, something that was real and exposed. Even though her moods weren't always pleasant or predictable, I trusted her to feel strongly and to say so. She brought raw life force into our house, and tenderness, and she was always true to her experience.

My father, on the other hand, was removed from extremes of feeling. He was friendly, with an easy way about him. He wasn't moved by sentimental films; nor did he cringe at the prospect of others' suffering. He was straightforward, taking the tender and painful challenges of being human in stride. I rarely saw him express anger or indignation. I only saw him cry one time when a good friend was killed in a trucking accident, and for a moment, he broke down while speaking at the funeral.

My father had learned early not to feel too much. Both of his parents and three of his five siblings had died by the time he was thirteen. After that, he grew up an orphan in the 1940s, played football, and, like most young men, was trained to go to war.

My dad didn't dwell in emotions, but he wasn't a robot either. There was freedom around him, a spaciousness you could count on, and a confidence that we could deal with life without the burden of emotional drama.

For intimacy and emotional closeness, I confided in my mother. But for the straightforward ability to face life as it came, my father was the best. I wouldn't want to choose between my mother's capacity to feel and my father's ability to ignore intense feelings. It would be like choosing between truth and beauty.

EMOTIONS ARE STATES

Every emotion is a state of consciousness, an experience composed of thought, mood, and bodily sensations. We refer to them as "states"[1] because they come and they go. They are not permanent, but rather pass through the body and awareness like a blustery storm in winter or a light breeze on a spring day. The problem with our emotions is that we don't relate to them as states. They don't just blow through our awareness. We hold on to them if they feel good, or we chase them away if they are painful. Lots of emotional states are uncomfortable. Anxiety can feel like nausea in the belly; boredom feels like a heavy weight you can't get out from under. We can dwell in painful emotional states, sometimes for days, unable to free ourselves or others from our bummed-out states of mind. Sometimes we attach so much to one emotion that it becomes a trait or an aspect of our character. We all know an "angry person" or "sad case." There are very difficult emotional processes like grief that take time. I'm talking about unconscious emotional patterns that we get stuck in.

Of course, we want to feel pleasurable emotions like excitement, joy, or mirth, and it is natural to want to minimize negative feeling states like worry, boredom, or disappointment. But feelings are meant to be felt. They are a potent source of information. They give depth to our experience, enriching our connections and bringing nuance and power to our shared experience. Would you want to only read novels that didn't evoke feelings or watch films that didn't move you? We want our emotions to be a doorway to empathize with others' suffering or to fire us up to work for social change. But we don't want to be trapped in them. We don't want to walk around in a habitual feeling as if we were wearing the same worn coat day in and day out, no matter what the weather. We want to be free to feel them completely and let go of them entirely.

TO INCLUDE AND EXCLUDE

"Emotional maturity" refers to the ability to feel fully, to be able to name and express our emotions, and to be open to receiving the feeling states in others. Including our emotions and expressing them well is an aspect of being human that takes intention and practice, which eventually ripens into a form of beauty. For some of us, the challenge is our estrangement from feeling. We have so disconnected from feeling that we fail to notice them at all. We can't expect to communicate about feelings when we don't seem to have them.

I have a young friend who is a recovering addict, and he is often alienated from his feelings, using substances as a way of dulling the pain and difficulty of his emotional life. Yesterday, an old friend called him for support, someone who is also trying to recover but relapsing frequently. They agreed to meet for the afternoon. But when the friend arrived, he was agitated and tense. He left quickly, probably to go get high. This left my young friend sad, bewildered, and, I think, mad. He told me about the incident, but when I asked him how he felt, he just muttered, "I don't know. It was weird."

I asked him how he felt. I tried to give him the space to think, to feel, and to consider his experience more directly while I listened. I asked him, "How do you feel about what happened? Do you feel sad that he is struggling so much? Did it make you mad that he came and then left abruptly like that? Do you wish you could have helped him?"

He said that more than anything he felt sad and powerless. He confessed he knows from the inside how hard it is to stop using drugs, and he saw himself in his friend. My friend has a challenge in learning to include his feelings, but he knows now that one critical aspect of recovery is learning to deal with pain and difficult emotions as they come up without numbing out.

The first step in becoming emotionally literate[2] is to simply begin to recognize feelings in the body. It is very helpful to work with a therapist or somatic healer who can coach you to identify and feel sensations, name feelings, and track the thoughts associated with them. When we explore our emotions like this, we learn to experience them directly. We locate them in the body, noticing their exact sensation and various qualities. We can feel a throb, an ache, or a tingle. We can feel the overall atmosphere of the emotion, naming dimensions of it like "tender," "sad," and "bewildered." We can see how our feelings are connected to thoughts and observe the story that goes along with them. We might be telling ourselves how someone let us down, misunderstood our motive, or a hundred other possibilities that give rise to a complex of feelings.

As we sit quietly and attentively, we learn to relax the mind and let go of the story that caused the emotion.

Then we are free to focus on the feelings themselves. We can engage the breath to create more openness and space so that we can experience the distinctive way feelings shift and change. Soon we experience anger as just passing through. It doesn't even feel like "my anger," and nothing is required of me. Different feelings come up and pass through, each simply expressing itself. They are like flowers blooming and fading away. They come and they go. They come and they go.

I am at a different stage of practice with my own emotions. Like my mother, I feel easily and strongly. I am adept at naming my feelings, even when they are complex. Rather than work at identifying my feelings, my practice is often to dis-identify with them—that is, to see them as "not me." Now when I have strong feeling reactions, I often let them go without expressing them. A strong meditation practice really helps me with this. But when sharing feelings can create more intimacy and depth in relationship, I want to express them.

DIVERSITY OF FEELINGS

Once after I had been upset with some politics at the office and had described it to my husband at dinner, Willie called to empathize with my feelings and left me a long, advice-filled voicemail message letting me know that "sometimes it just helps to get mad." He seems fascinated by my anger, and when he gets mad, he reminds me that he is "just like me."

I love Willie's empathy. In fact, I like it any time someone feels like I feel. But I am not always as gracious when someone feels differently than I do. If I feel anxious in a meeting, but my husband recalls how much he enjoyed it, I think he must be wrong. When my friend says she is angry about the upcoming election, but I feel excited, I wonder who is right. When my sister says she hasn't had a pang of nostalgia about selling the family home, I wonder how that can be when I am filled with acute sadness packing up old photos. I have to catch myself to keep from judging them as wrong or out of touch. It is vitally enriching to me to allow for differences in feeling responses. Just like we learn to include more than one perspective, learning to include more than one feeling response is another form of diversity.

THE PRACTICE

1. The next time you are in conversation, take time to include your feelings.

2. Ask the other person about how he or she feels.
3. Be curious about the differences in how you each feel.
4. Notice the richness of different sets of feelings as part of the conversational landscape.

TALKING ABOUT DIFFERENCE

Five Steps

*Beloved community is formed not by the
eradication of difference, but by its affirmation.*

—BELL HOOKS[1]

All of us are faced with situations that call for our differences to be addressed: that annoying disagreement
that comes up with our boss, an irritability in a marriage that persists, a cultural misunderstanding with a
friend. There comes a point when our ability to smooth
them doesn't go far enough. We end up in the territory described by our woman friend of "good as far as
it goes." Our relationships can be more trustworthy
when we learn to address our differences, even though
it can be awkward or stressful until we learn how. A

conversation that attempts to acknowledge and affirm difference, even when we can't negotiate it away, flatten it, or get rid of it, is a firm steppingstone toward more freedom and trust in all relationships.

As we have said, the body registers sameness and difference in different ways. When we agree, empathize, or just feel the same, there is a smooth quality in our conversations. They feel safe and easy. When we connect more deeply, making eye contact and listening intently, our conversations become deeply satisfying. Brain scientists say that when we humans connect with each other on a heartfelt level, the brain releases the hormone oxytocin,[2] which decreases anxiety and induces feelings of trust and empathy. Anytime we go deeply into a conversation, one imbued with feelings of calm and relaxation, oxytocin is probably flowing.

On the other hand, as we said earlier, even a small difference of opinion can cause the brain to trigger a whole series of reactions in our nervous system. Differences stimulate the nervous system and energize conversation. The adrenal glands release adrenaline, a stress hormone.[3] The heart starts thumping, and calmness and relaxation disappear. We feel a surge of energy with an impulse to move, along with increased focus and the ability to react. When differences are substantial, the body releases two other stress hormones: norepineph-rine and cortisol. Unlike the reduction in anxiety that oxytocin produces, the sensations brought about by the release of norepinephrine and cortisol start to feel uncomfortable as the excitement turns to agitation. It is particularly difficult to stay seated in conversation when these chemicals are releasing into our system, even in the smallest amounts, because they are designed to prime us for action and movement.

Instead of reacting to these sensations, which is what we tend to do, we can learn to befriend them. We can watch with interest how our differences stimulate conversation. We can pay attention to judgments when they come up, such as who is right and who is wrong, and how those judgments intensify our feelings of threat. If negative emotions, such as anger, jealousy, or pride, also arise, we can see how quickly these affect our view of our differences and help propel the differ-ences into deeper, more intractable conflicts.

The more familiar we are with the texture and range of sameness and difference in the body, the more skillfully we can work with them. In an exchange that unsettles or agitates us, for instance, we can smooth things out by creating more sameness. We can practice listening, ask an engaging question or two, focus on our shared values, or tell a funny story. All of these practices create relaxation, promoting harmony, ease, and a sense of belonging and togetherness.

But when discussions become sluggish, flat, or uninspiring, we can inject a dose of difference. Well-placed differences bring life to a conversation. They create contrast and spark energy. If the heat of the difference is moderated properly, the energy can fuel new perspectives and more depth in conversation. We can develop a taste for working with the disruptive energy. Like the hot pepper or splash of vinegar that enlivens a dull dish, we can add just the right amount of difference to keep our conversations and relationships energized and creative.

STEP ONE: PREPARE

It would be great if we could launch into a conversation any old time and it would go well. But like most things, taking a few minutes to prepare contributes to success, particularly if we are having strong feelings. Thinking ahead gives us a chance to calm down, prepare to listen, and clarify what we want to say. We can also clarify our thoughts and feelings. Is there anything we want from the other person? If we listen to ourselves first, it is easier to listen to the other person.

Preparing will also help us listen better. If we can think ahead about what the other person might say in the conversation, we can consider his or her perspective ahead of time. It is amazing how much more compassion we have when we simply consider what another point of view might be and what is right about it.

Then we can initiate the conversation. Usually, a good conversation begins with a question and a statement. An example might be, "I notice that you and I have a different working style. You seem to be very linear and sequential in how you get things done, while I am circular and organic in my approach. Have you noticed that? Would you agree? Is there anything you would suggest to help us integrate these differences?" Usually when you pose an issue, with a set of questions, you create an opportunity to practice listening.

STEP TWO: LISTEN

Keep in mind that when differences arise, they are exciting and stimulating, creating ripples in conversation and moments of charge or intensity in the body. That very stimulation makes it hard to listen. So it helps to prepare to listen, staying present to the body's response.

Keep in mind that listening doesn't mean agreement; it means listening. It is much harder to listen when we disagree or feel criticized. But remember that listening is a practice in sameness: being one with our own body and one with the person speaking. It is a good practice in allowing defensive sensations to simply circulate in the body. Until we know how to do that, the sensations can hijack the conversation. We close down, withdraw, or become sarcastic or aggressive in our response.

After listening, restate what you have heard, in a natural way. This brings clarity to the conversation, reassuring the other person that you have truly heard. Then ask the person what he or she heard you say. Don't mix listening with problem solving or negotiating. Wait until both of you have heard each other out to start the next step.

There are times when an extra dose of listening is really helpful. When someone is emotionally provoked, more listening will help the person calm down. When you are in a conversation in which you have more power (because you are the leader of a team, the boss of a company, or just the older sibling in the family), the tendency is to listen less. In fact, when in power, we should listen more, not less. If you are in a majority role, listening is a great ally to helping those in more marginalized roles express themselves more fully. If you are a man talking about gender, listen a little longer. If you are a white person, relax and let in other cultural perspectives. Anytime you can listen more, your conversation will probably go better. I want to reiterate that listening does not mean agreement. If you can keep that clear, your listening will improve.

STEP THREE: SHARE YOUR PERSPECTIVE

There are a couple of tried and true methods for sharing our perspective in a difficult conversation. Using first-person or "I" statements is the key. Saying "I am concerned about our working relationship" is different than saying "Our working relationship is a problem." The use of the third person asserts a truth and invites disagreement. The first person expresses a relative perspective and is easier to hear because it doesn't claim the position of truth.

Including our feeling states humanizes our communication and helps bring the heart online. Conceding that "I am angry" and taking responsibility for it without blame, or confessing that "I am sad," creates an emotional connection, as long as the feelings are free of blame. It can be very difficult to express the vulnerability in intimate conversations, but it is the most effective way to dissolve defensiveness on both sides.

Anytime we express our real thoughts and feelings, it creates more truth and reveals a bigger perspective. And anytime someone shares his or her truth with us, we should be grateful that we are given the opportunity to see and feel more than we did before.

STEP FOUR: RELAX AND WAIT

After a difficult conversation, it can be helpful to have a brief period of letting go and relaxing. Creative people understand that taking a break between generating ideas and finalizing them almost always results in a better outcome. Usually after we have talked, taking some down time, relaxing, and even meditating for a while creates an open space for a new insight to emerge. Sometimes we may not have time to wait or a solution erupts spontaneously while we talk. Then we should just go for it. Other times it is better to have the conversation and wait awhile before problem solving.

STEP FIVE: PROBLEM SOLVE

In any negotiation or problem-solving conversation, we need to express what we want and need, and what we want and need from the other side. Skillful negotiation involves seeing where our wants and needs overlap. We are usually surprised by how much more we have in common than we think. For example, in a work situation we might discover that we both want a good relationship, we both need efficiency in our work, and we can split the difference on who does what. Negotiation is inherently creative, and it can be fun to be surprised by fresh and interesting outcomes to our conflict.

Perhaps we resist engaging in challenging conversations because of our investment in the relationship. There are valuable people in our lives who also want to talk honestly, who want to take risks in communication, make mistakes, and learn. Over time, these relationships become more durable and trustable. The more we practice with these people, the better our skills and more efficient our conversations become. After a while, we become curious about differences, and conversations cease to be hard. Our relationships can be more trustworthy when we learn to address our differences simply and straightforwardly. Sometimes we can negotiate them and sometimes we have to learn to live with them. But in our attempt to acknowledge and affirm our differences, without heavy judgments and alienation, we are taking a big step toward greater freedom and fullness.

THE PRACTICE

Here is a simple recap of five easy steps to help you prepare when you face a difficult conversation.

1. Prepare to have the conversation by imagining the conversation you would like to have.
2. Listen. Summarize what you have heard.
3. Express your perspective, including feelings.
4. Relax and wait.
5. Problem solve. Share your ideas. Ask for the other person's.

NEGOTIATING WITH DAVID

*I'm doing what ancient people did. They had
really good reasons.*

—DAVID HOLLADAY[1]

David Holladay is my good friend, but we couldn't
be more different. We met for the first time when he
showed up on my front porch at my house in southern
Utah. I opened the door, and he was standing there,
looking like a character who had stepped straight out
of a magical realism novel. He wore a wide-brimmed
straw hat from Mexico, a long-sleeved shirt covered in
white chickens, a necklace made of dried red peppers,
and a handmade leather vest that went all the way to
his knees. He eyes were round, kind, and soft, and his
long hair was pulled back into a knot. His graying beard
looked like that of an old nineteenth-century patriarch.

David is a primitive skills expert who is famous in the Four Corners region. He knows the canyon lands intimately. He can live alone in the desert for weeks, foraging on grasshoppers, berries, and roots. He is truly wild, probably the only friend that I would use the word "undomesticated" to describe. Well, there are others, but no one I know is as proficient at living in the desert as he is.

Usually about once a year, we team up and lead excursions into the red rock country of southern Utah. For him, it is sharing his home, and for me, it is the best place by far to practice meditation. I spend most of my summers there, but I live the rest of the time in the city. When we work together, it is a study in contrasts.

Compared to David, I am very conventional and structured. For instance, I rely on my watch to keep time. I assume that this simple instrument will help me coordinate my efforts and actions. Not David. For him, the sun coming up in the early morning, rising high overhead at noon, and descending into the west at day's end is enough. If he needs to keep more precise track of time, he relies on a sundial. If he wants to know how many hours of daylight are left, he holds his fingers up against the horizon. Some days, he just feels his way with the light, arriving back in camp just as the sun is going down.

Our difference creates a few problems for us. Sometimes our timing is off, and we sometimes miss our intended rendezvous with each other. When we do finally meet up, I am usually the one who is upset and pointing to my Swiss watch and reprimanding him, "You were going to be here two hours ago!" Then he slowly responds to me, "Why are you upset? According to my time, we are right on schedule."

He explains that programs in nature should run without mechanical or digital devices. He points out that our trips are designed to help people take a break from technology. "People come to the desert to get away," he argues, "to get out of the city, park their cars, and put down their computers and cell phones. They are entitled to put it all down and spend their time looking up at the sky and feeling the light change without having their experience divided into minute increments with second hands ticking."

"But what happens when we need to rendezvous, David?" I protest. "What about coordinating to set up camp, prepare food, or meet somewhere in the mountains? What if there is an emergency? How do I know when to begin to be concerned? And how long do I wait for you to come back before I change plans?" He believes I should put away my watch and my self-righteous attitude and learn to read the light like he does.

POSITIONS

Ours is a very concrete difference. It doesn't always result in a conflict, but when it does, it appears unresolvable. In *Getting to Yes*,[2] the classic negotiation book, and one that I recommend, Roger Fisher and William Ury point out that when we commence a negotiation, we usually lead with our positions. My position is that workshop co-leaders need to use watches and clocks. It is obvious to me. His position is that in nature, leaders rely on the sun to tell time. From the perspective of our positions, the difference appears fixed and unresolvable.

The only way to work with this difference is to, first, simply respect it. As they like to say, "It is what it is." But this is challenging because we almost always attach a judgment to the difference. A judgment usually comes in the form of "I am right and you are wrong." Or "I am good and you are not quite as good." It is hard to experience a difference to be simply what it is—a difference. But when we have validated our differences and accorded them respect, we have created the solid groundwork to explore them.

INTERESTS

Once we have established the legitimacy of the difference, we can look underneath the position to interests. According to Fisher and Ury, interests are the real-life wants and needs that underlie the position we take. So the question becomes, "What is it that each person wants and needs from his or her position?" Asking this question is a leap of faith into the subjective territory of the difference. It is here, beneath the difference and the surface features of the position, that we are most likely to discover our commonality.

If I were to ask David what he wants and needs from going without a clock, he would probably say that he wants to wean people from their attachment to machines and technology. He would like to offer them the expansive experience of the daytime and the night, so they can feel time as a continuum, not broken up. Their activity can flow from this continuity seamlessly. He wants to allow them to flow with the movements of the earth, with the positions of the sun, moon, and stars, in the way our ancestors did. He hopes for them to enjoy the wholeness and fluidity of a day not broken up by discrete measurements. This natural beauty and cohesion really matter to him, and he likes giving them to other people.

My position is different than David's. So what are the wants and needs that underlie it? To begin with, David and I have very different roles in our retreat. He usually takes people out to the field, sometimes overnight, and I stay closer to our base camp leading early meditation, supporting the kitchen, or getting ready for an evening ceremony. I may take shorter excursions nearby, but I am doing hearth work mainly: taking care of people, food, and fire.

Coordination of the whole group is important to me. It is much easier to do my job when everyone is in sync. For example, I would like to make sure that if I take a group out on a short excursion from the camp, we are able to stay out as long as possible before returning. I don't want to bring my group back early only to find that David's group won't return for another two hours, or three, three-and-a-half, or four. I want to be sure the food is ready when people are back, so it doesn't get cold, and we have enough help with the dishes. I want to start a fire for a sweat lodge at the right time in the afternoon so the rocks are just right for the ceremony. A watch is, for me, shorthand for group cohesion, efficiency, and knowing when there might be a problem.

The key in any negotiation is to bring underlying sameness out of what appears to be an irresolvable difference. To get started with finding that common ground, we need to delve into what each party wants and needs from their position. Once the wants and needs are identified, we can begin looking for overlaps and similarities.

As the reader, you may take note of David's and my respective positions, and the wants and needs that underlie each of them. Do you still experience a wide chasm between us, or have you started to see that we may have more in common than it would appear? The word that jumps out for me most when I consider our common interests is "cohesion." I want the group to be coordinated and in flow with each participant, and David wants the group to be connected and flowing with the rhythms in nature. Since we both desire cohesion and being in nature in a way that is beautiful and seamless, identifying this shared interest provides the common ground for a fruitful conversation. We can see that we have the same basic values, and together, we have more of those values. Our other shared interests then fall neatly into place: safety, efficiency, and a good time. From an interests point of view, there is very little that we don't share.

OPTIONS

Now that we have identified our shared wants and needs, we can start to be creative about generating options that will meet our interests and close the gap of our difference. Taking a minute to brainstorm, can you come up with two or three ideas that you would suggest to David and me to help us out?

One suggestion that comes to my mind is that David try using a clock, but in a more limited way. Perhaps he would be willing to set an alarm at the end of his excursion, so he is aware when it is time to prepare to depart. Another idea would be that he use a clock to coordinate with me but not share it with participants. That way, bits of both worlds are at work.

If I were to offer an option from my side, I could switch from agreeing upon the exact hour of our rendezvous to a window of time that is more open-ended and flexible. Instead of 3 p.m., I could plan on 1 to 5 p.m. That way I would be free to stay in the field as long as I want before we meet up again.

We could also give the challenge to our group, soliciting their ideas for tracking time in a way that meets our shared values. What are their ideas for participating in the enterprise of staying coherent and moving in sync with each other? It is always amazing what a group can come up with when they are included in problem solving. Maybe we could even have a conversation about how two different groups can keep time with and for each other—with or without a clock.

So you can see that once we get past the positions and begin to access the underlying interests, we see how much we have in common. We don't need to get rid of the difference; we couldn't even if we tried. Rather, we can reach below it to find the wants and needs being served by it. In this case, a difference that started out to be alienating, problematic, and divisive now became the source of a deeper conversation that built cohesion between us, our participants, and our time in nature.

THE PRACTICE

1. Notice a conflict or difference in your life right now that needs to be worked out.
2. Take up your own position. Now look below your position to your wants and needs. What are they, and how are they satisfied by your position?

3. Now take the position of the other side. Think about what they want and need from their position.
4. As you explore wants and needs, where do they overlap? What do you have in common?

THE GREAT DIVIDE

Conflict

I am at peace with God. My conflict is with man.
—CHARLIE CHAPLIN AS
MONSIEUR VERDOUX[1]

We all have moments in our lives when a difference erupts into a conflict. My viewpoint inevitably runs headlong into your viewpoint, like my car sometimes backs into another one in a parking lot. Sometimes our collisions are small, nothing more than momentary divisions; other times they are the extended disruptions that provoke change. Rather than viewing them as wrong, however, we can view our everyday collisions as opportunities for change, growth, and even for new levels of intimacy.

Conflicts fuel our personal development because they are naturally filled with tension and catalyzing energy. They force us to confront things that aren't working. We tend not to change unless something powerful compels us out of the comfortable status quo and into a new way of being.

People make jokes these days about not wanting to be presented with another "learning opportunity," and that reluctance is reasonable. Life is always more than challenging, requiring us to change and adapt, to learn new things, and to keep up with the latest trends, research, and information. But sometimes it is the natural unfolding of our own development that prompts us to learn a new skill set. In other words, we seem designed to grow, and in the course of those changes, new perspectives emerge and new skills are required.

With time, our attitude toward conflict changes. We begin to see conflicts as just an exaggerated difference. They don't have to result in ongoing quarrels or estrangements. We may still feel threatened in moments that never seem to go away, but we have the courage to work with the conflict directly, trusting the innate intelligence of the struggle.

Recently, I experienced a conflict of this kind in my own community. We were in the process of building a meditation center—a simple, elegant structure in the red rocks of the Utah desert. The effort was led by a committee made up of people with different skill sets, such as building expertise, artistic ability, and sustainability values. We had made steady progress in raising money and getting the architectural plans drawn up. Everything was moving along swimmingly until we encountered the question of what kind of heating and cooling system to use. Then we got our wheel stuck in a ditch.

Several members wanted to work with a traditional heating system, buying electricity from the local power company. They argued that the system was simple, reliable, easy to maintain, and inexpensive. This seemed pretty straightforward until several other members said no. They wanted us to make a change to the status quo, get off the fossil fuel habit and onto the green bandwagon. They advocated use of a system that generated heat from solar panels and hot water. "Why," they argued, "would we participate in the archaic burning of coal when we could get off the grid and free our new building of a carbon footprint altogether? In this perilous time of climate change," they said, "we have an ethical obligation to sustainability, even though the new system would require more learning, would certainly be more complicated to maintain, and would cost more money up front."

At first I imagined an easy compromise, but that didn't happen. People were righteously committed to their perspectives, stubborn really, and nobody seemed willing to budge. I found myself becoming irritated with our group and negatively judging people on both sides of the argument.

Luckily a new perspective occurred to me. This conflict was exactly the conflict we needed to have. It pushed us right up against the biggest challenge of our time and demanded that we consider the exact issues that human culture is grappling with all around the globe. Why should we expect to be exempt from the struggle of change? In other words, our difference is a most worthy one, shared by people the world over right now and deserving of our attention, our struggle, the challenges we put to each other.

From then on, my relationship to the conflict changed, and I stopped making everyone wrong and started instead to trust our goodwill and our chance to work it out. Together, we decided to install a system that can be converted to solar as soon as our funding can support the transition. Everyone was happy enough with the outcome.

It is a very freeing experience to suddenly realize that a difference between us is not only OK, but it is also intelligent and worthwhile. This realization heightens our confidence to bring out our differences directly and openly. Once we do, we can learn how to navigate them more efficiently. There is less dread, less shame, and less blame. Instead of taking hours and days to talk something over, we can take minutes to work something out because we trust the process and each other.

When I ask my students to reflect on what they would like to change about their relationship to conflict, they say:

I would like to feel less afraid when a conflict arises.
I usually respond defensively, and I want to change that.
I want to be able to take a stand for my true position. My self-worth depends on it.
I want to speak more honestly about what I really think and feel.
I want to learn to listen, but it is hard for me.
I would like to be curious and ask a question rather than immediately justifying my viewpoint.
I judge other people who are different from me as

wrong. There must be another way to see things.
I would like to be genuinely open to other people's
　　perspectives and ideas, instead of always
　　defending myself and my position.
People tell me that I am too angry. I would like to
　　manage my emotions better.
I don't want to die the way my parents did—
　　stuck in old patterns, embittered, unable to
　　communicate about what most matters to me.

Their desire to grow into a new way of being is natural. They are curious about something they sense is possible but they haven't yet experienced. Or conversely, they spontaneously long to outgrow a way of being that no longer serves them. But these aspirations require a new skill set, so the natural growth also involves some hard work. (See *Everything Is Workable*.) We must learn to see conflict not as a problem to be solved, but an opportunity to be engaged. What appears to us as irresolvable conflict is really a creative possibility in a "distressing disguise," to use Mother Teresa's words.[2]

We can learn to change our patterns and turn toward conflict, but this willingness to lean in is counterintuitive. It is like the pilot who has learned to overcome gut instincts and rely on instruments during a storm, because he or she knows that those instincts can't be trusted at ten thousand feet in rough conditions. When we lean toward conflict, we are literally overriding our oldest, deepest protective habits. Turning toward conflict will engender change; by engaging in it, working with it, we, paradoxically, become freer.

If a conflict arises in a relationship, it might be time for a talk. Or it could be an opportunity to make a change. When things are stirred up and the status quo isn't working anymore, a conflict won't let us rest until we do something differently. Sometimes relationships need to change; sometimes our context or work needs to change. Sometimes we ourselves need to change.

Finally, conflict is a way for us to learn how to integrate our differences. As we learn to include more difference, our relationships become more interesting, more authentic, more trustable. We have more bandwidth for the challenge of being human, and we can engage that challenge together.

THE PRACTICE

Complete these sentences:

1. When I hear the word "conflict," I . . .

2. When a conflict arises, my body . . .
3. In my family when a conflict arose, we . . .
4. If I could change one thing about myself in dealing with conflict, I would . . .

11

DIFFERENCES IN STYLE

Style is the difference,
a way of doing, a way of being done.
—CHARLES BUKOWSKI[1]

Willie's most powerful gift is being. He knows how to be, plain and simple. He called me up recently and said, "I am just happy, you know." I asked him, "What is it that is making you so happy?" And he said, "It's my own." Willie's happiness is not usually based on what he did today. It doesn't depend on how he is seen by others or on an idea of how things should be. It comes simply and directly from his being. He has a quiet bliss about him that rises up from his simplicity.

I love Willie's differences. They wake me up. Recently, we were visiting my mother, and she asked him if he was interested in getting a job. I thought it was a good question for her to pose to her young grandson. I perked up, interested in what he would say. He replied only, "I like my life." He didn't respond defensively like I would have; he didn't feel criticized. He didn't even for a moment consider the idea that he should get a job. He just explained that he likes everything the way it is. This took me and my mother both by surprise, leaving us without advice or a reprimand. Enough said.

Willie is not always in a good mood. Just like the rest of us, he can feel threatened, defensive, or reactive. His anxiety usually takes the form of dead weight. He becomes so stubborn and immovable that he seems aligned with the great force of gravity itself. I remember once when Willie was about twelve, he was part of a New Year's program at the mall downtown. At midnight, he was supposed to go up on the stage and make a New Year's resolution. He became so anxious while we were waiting that his body became heavier and heavier and heavier, until he literally slid down the wall into a heap on the ground.

You can't reason with Willie when he is in this state. You can't comfort him either because he stops communicating altogether. He becomes extremely dense. As my aunt used to say, "He is a hard dog to get off the porch." He just hunkers down. So with little time to spare, I gave a quick shout, commanding him to get up and go up to the stage. I didn't deliver a personal attack; it was more like a military directive to help cut through his heaviness. He made it up and onto the stage and delivered his New Year's bit just fine. And he was happy he did. This is an example of how our differences can meet up and allow us to help each other. My clarity and sharpness sometimes serve him; his relaxation and innate well-being are healing for me.

In Buddhist terms, Willie belongs to one of five different energetic styles called the five wisdom energies.[2] The five wisdom energies are sometimes referred to as "wisdom families," and include the *vajra*, *buddha*, *ratna*, *karma*, and *padma* style. Each describes different patterns of energy, ways of being, and styles of relating with the world. Each style includes a particular kind of intelligence and the problems each one suffers when the protective mechanism of the ego appropriates it. When I was first introduced to this teaching in my early twenties, I found it extremely helpful. I stopped assuming other people were just like me; instead I became curious about the real differences between us. I learned to respect the strengths and the weaknesses of each style. For me, this teaching on differences was a form of compassion. It helped me to be kinder.

ALL-ACCOMMODATING WISDOM

The buddha energetic style is known for its wide-open spaciousness, its love of being, and like Willie, its ability to appreciate things as they are. Someone with this style of energy doesn't need anything special to happen. They genuinely feel that things are sufficient as they are. Nothing needs to be added; nothing needs to be changed. Buddha family types are, for the most part, less judgmental and less demanding than people from the other families. In fact, they provide an open space in which other people feel free to be themselves. Willie is like this. I can't recall him ever saying that someone should be different than they are. When he was distressed about a friend who had recently disappeared from our life due to his drug use, I asked him how he felt. He said, "I am waiting for him to come back to his real self."

When used as a defense, however, this natural tolerance can become a form of ignorance. A buddha family type will often space out instead of speaking up, let things be when action is needed, or utter "all good" instead of demanding change. We don't often think of tolerance as a form of ego-defense, but for the buddha family style, this open space becomes like a cloud that the person can hide out in, and like all the families, the wisdom turns to neurosis when the ego gets involved.

MIRRORLIKE WISDOM

I am known for my precision of my mind, my clarity, and my ability to cut through confusion and make things clear. On the other hand, when I feel threatened or defensive, I am also known to be sharp, irritable, and sometimes aggressive. In the five wisdoms teaching, my energy is referred to as the vajra style. In Sanskrit, this means "diamond" or "thunderbolt." The vajra quality is clear, reflecting precisely and accurately like a mirror. People with this style have a gift for seeing things in great detail and with immense precision. A vajra family person can see a large, panoramic viewpoint or take a metaperspective easily. Since these people have access to a big perspective, they are often visionary, providing a map that helps us see more clearly where we are and where we are headed.

My brilliant friend and teacher Ken Wilber is a true genius of the vajra family. In his writing, he provides an extremely clear and detailed map that describes the evolution of human culture and the development of human beings, especially spiritually. He never confuses the map with the real territory that must be lived and navigated, although sometimes other people do. His conceptual maps offer clarity, a sense of relief, and guidance for many seekers. In Ken Wilber's writing, he clearly sets forth the idea that anyone interested in growth and awakening should include exploring differences in type because engaging the tension of our differences creates health and vitality in our lives.[3]

Vajra types can be extremely principled because they can draw lines and set boundaries more easily than other styles. People with this gift are capable of tremendous integrity. They have a natural inclination toward ethical conduct, as well as a strong sense of decorum, of what is appropriate and what isn't. They can be clear thinkers who love analysis, philosophy, and mathematics. Indeed, they are the insightful "knowers" of the five families, extremely detailed and precise, as long as they don't become hardened know-it-alls.

As a form of protection, however, the clarity of the vajra family can lead to being overly critical or self-righteous. They also have a habit of getting angry easily. This problem arises for me when I am so clear that I feel I am automatically right about things. This can mean that everyone should see what I see, and it follows that they should do what I want them to do.

And when they don't, I am mad about it. I lose the big picture and contract into my narrow viewpoint and then impose it on others. My clarity becomes dogmatic, my decorum becomes rigid, and my precision is uptight. There can also be a sense of superiority or arrogance in the vajra family, and I have gotten that feedback before. Once, I think. No, seriously, this is the basic problem with the ego's impulse toward self-protection. I can quickly lose my connection to the whole and then act righteous about it.

THE WISDOM OF EQUANIMITY

My friend Jay is a member of the ratna family. *Ratna* translated from Sanskrit means "jewel," and is an expression of wealth, of richness and abundance. That is the world my friend lives in. His presence is robust and welcoming; his activity is very nurturing. He has a "mi casa es su casa" attitude. He doesn't have a lot of money, but I feel enriched just walking into his home. He loves his comfort, his pleasure, and his sensual appetites. Even better, he loves to share all of it. His relaxation, unlike Willie's (which comes from deep in his being), emanates from having more than enough. He is the consummate host, offering equanimity, enrichment, and a house of plenty to his friends.

I often go visit him at the end of the day when the light is mellowing and when the day is wrapping up. It is a time to slow down, to appreciate completion, and to enjoy the sun setting over his garden, which is ripe with tomatoes, squash, and hefty pumpkins. I spend some time enjoying the garden and then come to the kitchen, where the walls are painted in warm hues of yellow, rose, and olive green with pictures of Italy and the Amalfi Coast hanging on them. He always has one or two bottles of wine on the counter and pours a glass while praising me for coming by. There are various cheeses on the counter—Gorgonzola, Stilton, and Gruyère—and an array of whole bread and crackers, as well as olives, artichokes, red peppers, and figs. Sometimes there is a pan of fish on the stove or a pot of bean soup simmering. Generosity is, without a doubt, his most enlightened virtue and hospitality his truest gift. Oh yes, I almost forgot. He always has some chocolate or ice cream in the fridge. Just when you think it is over, there is more.

But like Willie and me and everybody else, the ratna person also has bouts of anxiety and dread. But these states look different; they follow a ratna pattern. They are not sharp like mine or dull like Willie's. When the ego is threatened in this style, generosity contracts, and the air of abundance shrinks to insufficiency. All of a sudden, there isn't enough and there never will be enough. The ratna type feels empty and unsatisfied, and reaches out for more. It could be food or drink or trips to the shopping mall. It doesn't really matter. There is an impulse to try to fill up an empty feeling. This compulsive grasping becomes greed for people in the ratna family. The fullness of the ratna type can vacillate between inflation and depletion. People's egos can also get a little too big, overfull, exaggerated, even prideful. Like all the families, the innate gift, when filled with anxiety, becomes an obstacle to living openly and freely.

ENLIGHTENED ACTIVITY

My sister is a force of nature. She is a radio host, a celebrity in her hometown of Portland, Oregon, and a woman who knows how to get things done. Once, I was at her home with a friend of mine who had never met her before. Soon she strode in in her four- or five-inch heels, which she wears every day, even though she is already five feet ten. Having just come from work, she said a friendly hello to my friend in passing and then stepped up onto a dining chair and right up onto the table. Then she stood there in the middle of the dining room table, reaching high over her head in her skinny jeans with her belly exposed, changing a lightbulb while continuing the conversation. My friend says she will never forget meeting her. It was an event.

My sister belongs to the karma family. This is the energetic type of person who embodies enlightened activity. She naturally knows what to do and how to get it done. Being with her is like being in strong wind. There is purpose, direction, and always movement. She is fun. When we were younger, even though I was older than her, she took me shopping or skiing or boating or hiking or to the movies. She loved activity and staying busy, while I was more introverted: contemplative, pondering life, being human, and the fact that we die. Later, I learned to meditate, and she developed an impressive career in broadcast journalism.

There is great beauty and intelligence in my sister, and she can be counted on in ways few people can to do what she says she will. The gift of karma family people is that they are competent and efficient. These qualities are of extreme benefit to others. They have excellent timing and know how to let a situation ripen until the moment for action. The element of the karma energy is the wind, and when they are at their best, things seem to get done with no effort at all.

The problem arises when *doing* isn't the answer to what is needed in the circumstances. Karma people will often overdo the doing, failing to slow down and make contact with themselves, with others, and with life. Sitting still provokes anxiety; so do long conversations with no goal in sight. Karma people sometimes appear frantic, unsettled, or unnecessarily busy. In the extreme, they chase after a goal or an image but may fail to live wholeheartedly along the way. There is a funny bumper sticker that reminds me of the karma type's approach to life: "Jesus is coming. Look busy."

Even though my sister and I have a tendency to judge each other and to compete like sisters will, we genuinely appreciate our differences and what each one offers to the other. She does an unexpected favor for me, scheduling an interview for me on her television station, and I give her advice about dealing with an emotional tangle she is in. The beauty of family is knowing how significant the differences are and learning to appreciate them, while seeing how deep and lasting our sameness really is.

DISCRIMINATING AWARENESS

The final wisdom energy is the padma style. *Padma* means "lotus" in Sanskrit, and the padma's element is fire. Padmas are all about passion, intimacy, seduction, and beauty. Think of Bill Clinton. He is a charming, charismatic force of nature. I have heard that when he connects with you, you feel as if you are the only person in a room of five hundred. He is known to be a profound listener and a smooth talker. But his skill in making human contact is, as we all know, sometimes to his own detriment and to the country's. The downside of the padma style is that they can be addicted to seduction and are easily magnetized to a new person or another enticing situation. So they can be quite quixotic, chaotic, and sometimes unfaithful.

The padma person's gift is his or her discriminating awareness, the ability to see in detail and to appreciate the subtle difference between this and that. For example, the ratna mother will create beautiful meals for all of her children and family; there is a great sense of belonging and wholeness; while the padma mother will attend to each one of her children's particular likes and dislikes. Padma people have a gift for making things special.

They make very good therapists and teachers, as well as satisfying intimate partners, because they are so good at giving an experience of being seen and heard by others. They can also be demanding because they want to feel connected at all times. But that same demand makes them excellent entertainers and artists who are good at expressing themselves because they are so connected to the phenomenal world and to their audience. They can paint it, dance it, or sing it, and you will feel it.

The padma type is deeply connected to the heart, so they mean it when they ask, "How are you?" Being so connected to the world creates vulnerability in them. They are touched, and their hearts are easily broken. They have a tendency to be emotionally needy, to feel incomplete without intimate contact, and often suffer from loneliness and nostalgia more than the other styles. They are more likely to be enmeshed with others and entangled in the human drama. On the other hand, because of the connection to the heart, padma types have tremendous compassion. When Bill Clinton advocates for people of color, it comes from his relationships growing up with African Americans in the South, and his care for black culture is deep and real. He has a thousand flaws, but his compassion is not one of them.

Hillary has lived with Bill all these years, in spite of his infidelities. She is often criticized for it, but on the other hand, I can imagine that she loves having coffee with the guy in the morning, reading the *New York Times* together, and listening to the Sunday news shows. I bet there is no one she would rather talk to about foreign policy or mapping out a campaign strategy. Most importantly, they have a daughter together and a grandchild, as well as years and years of shared purpose and history. If they hadn't been together, they wouldn't have their differences. Their love for each other is the source of their pain. The closer we are to someone, the more we suffer that person. Real intimacy is the same and very different.

THE PRACTICE

1. Think about a person you are close to.
2. What are his or her special gifts?
3. What talents does this person have that are unlike yours?
4. When this person is scared or threatened, does that same gift become an obstacle in relationship?
5. Can you appreciate this person for his or her strengths and weaknesses?

YOU AND ME, US AND THEM

Us and them
And after all we're only ordinary men
Me and you
God only knows it's not what we would choose to do
—PINK FLOYD[1]

I used to be a communications and relationship missionary. I was so inspired to develop my skills; I imagined everyone else would be too. I quickly learned they didn't feel like I did. Maybe they were naturally at ease in their relationships and weren't suffering like I was. Or maybe they already had a depth of connection and authenticity that didn't require practice. Or maybe they just weren't as affected by the differences, the misunderstandings, or the strange and confusing communications that ruffled my feathers.

In the last ten years, I have been very influenced by the work of Ken Wilber and his colleagues who study and teach adult developmental psychology.[2] He has changed how I think about relationship skills development, pointing out that the desire to include different perspectives, to listen, to question, and to doubt yourself varies at different levels of adult development. As our ability to take perspectives changes, our view of the world changes, and so does our way of communicating about it. This developmental framework helps to explain to me much of the confused communications that I see on television and in the media, where people seem to go to great lengths to completely miss one another's message. It also helped me to clarify my own communications, finding better ways to express myself and to understand others.

Using an adult developmental framework to look at differences can show us real possibilities, and also limits, in relationship. Take, for example, someone who is egocentric from a developmental point of view. In the conventional sense of the word, "egocentric" means "self-centered." We all have a part of us like that. We want things the way we want them. We have an inner infant who will throw a temper tantrum or sulk to get our own way. In a certain place, in a certain mood, or under certain circumstances, we simply do not want to include the wants and needs of others, like maybe sometimes when we've not eaten yet and are really hungry. This is not a particularly pleasant state of mind. Usually it is a little bit desperate because from an egocentric perspective, everyone else is an "other." I know what it feels like; I'm sure you do, too. For most of us, self-centeredness is a temporary mood; it happens under stress or pressure of some kind.

Yet, when we look around, we see lots of examples of people for whom this is not a temporary state. It is a character trait. We might see a drug dealer selling an addict his or her next fix, both utterly blind to their mutual destructiveness. We might see this at work when our boss repeatedly says he wants input and then punishes people for giving it. Or it may come up at a family gathering when a sibling gets up and storms off, incapable of a challenge to his or her viewpoint. We can probably all think of someone in our life who cannot consider the perspective of others because this person's own viewpoint takes up the full bandwidth of his or her awareness.

The sad truth is that this self-concern might stem from an early life that was unsafe, trauma filled, chaotic, or neglectful. Now it seems as if the egocentric person must promote his or her interests at all times in order to survive. But the person is isolated at a deep level, making it almost impossible to have a real relationship with others. True egocentrism is a form of suffering. It wouldn't occur to the fundamentally egocentric person to work on relationship skills because such a person doesn't have the free attention to tune into another viewpoint. From a psychological perspective, this might be labeled "narcissism,"[3] depending on how deep the egocentrism runs in the character structure of the individual. But it is a form of a difference that can be tough to overcome in relationship.

ETHNOCENTRIC

Most of us move beyond our self orientation to the ethnocentric level. In other words, we expand to find support, safety, and identity in our family and group. We are able to put our immediate needs on hold for someone we love or to adapt our preferences to keep harmony in our tribe. I am reminded of a conversation that I had with an at-risk youth who told me proudly that he liked his boss so much that he wouldn't steal from him, even though it would be easy. It struck me as strange, but from a developmental point of view, his perspective had grown from egocentric to ethnocentric and now included loyalty to his boss.

From this wider socialized vantage point, we genuinely want to consider those around us. We are willing to conform in dress, speech, and conduct, and contribute to the group purpose. We value duty and loyalty, and will sacrifice ourselves and our preferences for the good of the whole. Belonging and harmony at a socialized level of development is not only a true value, according to Susanne Cook-Greuter, "It is an achievement."[4] Our relationships at this level are based on willingness to cultivate sameness, not difference.

There is a strong boundary at an ethnocentric level just like there is at an egocentric level. But at this level, the boundary runs between "us and them," instead of "you and me." Being on the inside of it, and not on the outside, is important for safety's sake. In this context, we submit to the rules and conventions, and understand our safety, even our salvation, to be within this context and these people. If we are going to war, these are the ones we will fight and die for. And after the war is over, if we make it, there is a lasting bond between us and the people with whom we served.

When push comes to shove, ethnocentrism means we support and protect those who are like us. For example, we will close the borders, insist that everyone speak one language, and demand that you are for us or against us. In the political arena, both Democrats and Republicans may be ethnocentric or not. If they think all the other party is totally wrong about everything all the time, chances are they see through an ethnocentric lens, which is black and white. And by the way, we are all ethnocentric; it is just a question of how deep and how often.

The beauty of ethnocentrism is the very strength of the boundary between us and them. There is a clear inside and a clear outside. Everybody knows who belongs and who doesn't. Everyone also knows when a baby is born or when someone has died. Rites of passage, ceremonies, and ritual acts are important in the group. Everybody makes an effort to go to weddings and funerals. They bring a gift and express appreciation, or they bring flowers and express condolences. People make gestures of loyalty to the community, and it is a value that is not taken for granted.

There may come a point in a developmental scheme when an ethnocentric worldview is too confining, too conformist, or too tight to grow in. If that happens, we have two choices. We have to find a way to stay the same or find a way to change. Change comes about when the cultural conformity limits our ability to ask real questions or explore real issues, and the tension that comes from crossing the boundary is less painful than the stagnation caused by staying the same. It might occur when we get really curious about what is going on over the fence or over the next horizon. We want to see beyond the boundaries and safety of our group. We decide to travel or to move on. We want to see the world. There is an excitement in the move from ethnocentric to world-centric because difference is no longer frightening. It is stimulating.

WORLD-CENTRIC

So we expand our perspective and move into a world-centric space. Once again, it is more spacious, and the boundaries around self and other change again. They now include me, us, and all of us. We still value sameness, but not with our local group, with our shared humanity. To do this, however, we must consider the very real cultural, religious, and race differences between us. In other words, our desire for sameness necessitates including differences because they can't be flattened or overlooked. In the same way that the brain differentiates and then creates connection through the differences,[5] the world-centric person becomes capable of including and integrating differences with other humans. More importantly, we can tolerate the tension that comes from sustaining an encounter with those from another tribe.

I have a student who has a dual passport, Gabriel Wilson. He is American and Brazilian. His father is from Saint Louis, and his mother is from Rio de Janeiro. He grew up in the States until he was eight and then moved to Rio until he finished high school and came back to the United States for college. He is truly bicultural, and he has a world-centric perspective that I can count on—that is, until the subject of soccer comes up. And then, forget about it. He is Brazilian all the way. He is quick to ask, "Now how many times has the United States beat Brazil in soccer?" And then he answers his own question: "Oh, right, just that one lonely time."

"Overall score: Brazil, 16; United States, 1. Boom."

Gotta love that ethnocentrism!

Belonging to two cultures catapults you to a world-centric level. From this vantage point, soccer aside, we appreciate the gifts of both cultures and the serious problems that each has. It is easy to see that our fates are all linked, and it is imperative that we put our respective skills on the table, ready to walk toward our future challenges together. We can find a way to honor our differences and join together in shared vision and higher values.

In another conversation about the world-centric perspective, a French gay man related how when growing up, he felt quite victimized by his sexual orientation. Later after having moved to the United States, he discovered that in a different context, he was not the victim; he was the oppressor. This was because others identified him as a white man with privilege, a role he had never identified with before. But he could see how both were equally true. He said it is like looking at more than just two stars, a whole series of stars. Suddenly there was a picture of a multipolar connection of oppressors and victims running throughout cultures and history. In the end, he said, we are so connected; there is no way we cannot be oppressor, as well as a victim. But this is the perspective of a world-centric person. It may not be a lens that someone else can see through.

When we move to world-centric, we glimpse the interplay of the systems we live and participate in. Everything we do depends not just on other people, but on living in a peaceful country, on infrastructures that work, on economic systems that don't break down. It is completely apparent that we don't accomplish things on our own. Even more, we want to see the reasons and causes why things are the way they are, and we have confidence that we can change them. We want to make the world a better place. We feel for the whole of humanity and see the inequities in the world much more clearly. We improve our own life by stepping out, and we are sure we can do it together.

At this stage, exploring differences appears necessary and compelling. Before, we were simply coping with our different viewpoints, but now there is a real interest in exploring alternative perspectives. We see that just as you came from a culture background, early life, and family history completely your own, so did I. And we recognize, maybe for the first time, neither of us is entirely right, and neither of us is entirely wrong. All of our previous black-and-white thinking softens, taking on shades of gray. We see different, multiple interpretations and a variety of perspectives interacting. We have a genuine interest in examining our different underlying beliefs and assumptions. This takes some courage, but it is also very exciting.

At a world-centric level, we want to include every perspective and see the truth in it.[6] We start to see everyone as a little bit right, which changes our dynamic with the world and our differences forever. In fact, we can become fascinated by the dynamism of diversity. But we can encounter a huge frustration trying to figure out how to pull all those perspectives together, so that a pattern of deep cohesion and trust can stabilize to include these differences. Luckily, as we include more perspectives, we also seem to develop more patience. We move from a short-term attitude of "Let's get it solved now" to a much longer view. We now have patience to allow differences to morph and change, and for solutions to eventually emerge. Our concern about the human condition is matched by our trust in our own unfolding.

KOSMIC-CENTRIC

As our perspectives increase, so do our problems. They grow in size from egocentric issues to ethnocentric concerns to world-centric threats. They seem to get bigger and bigger and bigger. At world-centric, there is no longer an "other" in the same way. We identify with humanity and all life on the planet. But it seems like our global issues have become our enemy, an enormous "other" that we are constantly fearing and worrying about. Temperature increases, disparity among rich and poor, political unrest and violence, human trafficking networks that span many countries, a great swirling island of plastic in the Pacific Ocean.

With challenges this immense, we need an even bigger perspective. But how do we access a vantage point large enough to deal with the fear and over-whelmingness of the pressures of an entire globe? It is hard to fathom a shift so radical, but they say it happens often when astronauts go to space. As they pass out of the atmosphere and turn to look back at the beautiful sphere of earth hanging silently in the dark, something truly wonderful happens. It is called the "overview effect,"[7] a total shift in perspective and attitude. From space, national boundaries dissolve, the conflicts that divide us are invisible, and the unity that is our shared existence is obvious and touching. Many astronauts report an overwhelming experience of love for the planet, for humanity, and for all of life together after viewing the singular, blue-and-white orb suspended in the silence.

We can call this a kosmic-centric perspective,[8] and I use Ken Wilber's spelling to indicate that the shift in perception affects us inside, as well as outside. It is a shift that occurs when the boundary between me and you, us and them, and humanity and all the rest dissolves. From this point of view, there is no fixed boundary. Reality is as it is. Complete. Continuous. Whole. Including all life and even death. Most importantly, because there is no boundary, we are no longer separate or other. We have a sense of recognition, of being at home, and of utterly belonging.

This shift can occur in many ways. Some people experience it unexpectedly when their first child is born or glimpse it after a near-death experience. It can happen suddenly after ingesting a dose of LSD or psilocybin mushrooms. Sometimes it occurs spontaneously, unexpectedly, or in the aftermath of great suffering. Many people experience this after a period of intense practice meditating or gradually over time, through steady dedication to prayer and service.

However the shift comes about, our entire relationship to space and time seems to change, as well as our relationship to ourselves. For the first time, there is no inside or outside, no you and me, no us and them. For the first time, the division between past and future disappears, and awareness is fully present in the here and now. Resting open and alert, there is a pervasive, emotional calm, a feeling of serenity and stillness. Right here and right now, everything is as it is—completely sufficient.

It is difficult to describe this shift until one experiences it, but it is real. It is incredibly vivid. Because attention is right here, right now, our eyes see color and shape more vividly, our ears pick up the tiniest sound, and the full detail of each moment is real and apparent. We know that our life is as unique as it is precious. And we know it is changing. We embrace the mystery of our life and death, but somehow, it isn't as frightening anymore. As Jack Kerouac says in the novel *Dharma Bums*, "How strange, how worthy, how good for us."[9]

For the first time, fear doesn't dominate our body and mind. We are not simply managing our egoic boundaries, our agitated nervous systems, and our tenuous relationships. There is a deep relaxation with existence and an ability to see the beauty of both chaos and order, and of life and death. Both sides are part of one seamless whole. Our self-identity has expanded to the point that the labels egocentric, ethnocentric, world-centric, and even kosmic-centric won't contain who I am. I just am.

With this enormous shift in perspective, the heart seems to naturally open to include everything. A great kindness sets in. We feel love for all beings. Our problems are still immense, and perhaps unsolvable, but we can engage with them. We love life and the world, but we lose the arrogance that insists we can push our way to an easy solution. We understand that reality is much bigger than we are, and the only way forward is to humbly be part of it. We can't control it, but we can be in relationship to it.

We learn to become less attached to a particular solution to our problems. Rather, we participate in a vision about what may be possible. We are keenly aware that we are part of a process unfolding and that, moment to moment, we need to do our part. But we can't stay in a dualistic understanding that excludes low from high, death from life, failure from success. We see it is all part of this outrageous miracle we are part of. Maybe there is everything to do, and maybe nothing at all. But whatever we do, it becomes imperative to do it kindly and in an openhearted way, even when things are dire.

From the kosmic-centric perspective, we can look at all of our challenges at each level. How does the refugee crisis look from space? How does the world-centric perspective change our view of natural systems, and how does it allow us to work across national boundaries? What insights from the ethnocentric perspective will help communities preserve their culture in a healthy way? And from a kosmic-centric perspective, how does the egocentric self need compassion and support to care for itself? It is all of a piece.

You can feel this kosmic-centric perspective in some of our global leaders. When Nelson Mandela was leading South Africa after apartheid, he was gracious and kind, even though he was imprisoned for almost thirty years. You could feel his heart, hear it when he talked; you could see it in his smile. You can feel it in His Holiness the Dalai Lama, too, and in Aung San Suu Kyi. They are not only politically adept; they are spiritually evolved. They are models for the kind of activists we can be when we develop ourselves and let reality rule. Our task is to open up the widest possible perspective and allow it to inform all the details and the differences. In doing so, we serve me, us, all of us, and all of it.

THE PRACTICE

1. Reflect for a moment on your ego identity. What do you notice about it? What are your fears and desires?

2. Now reflect on your ethnocentric identity. How does your perception shift? What becomes important now?

3. Can you experience yourself as world-centric? What hopes do you have? What concerns?

4. Can you identify as the kosmic-centric self? How big are you? Can you find a limit? What do you care about?

5. Now look at your ego from this point of view. Look at your family. And the world.

6. Does anything appear different to you now?

13

FREE FROM IDENTITY

People may be Northerners or Southerners.
But in True Nature, there can be no North or South.
—ZEN MASTER HUI-NENG[1]

One day, I was at the salon getting my hair cut. Willie had gone with me and was doing what he does so well—sitting and chilling, just hanging out in a chair opposite me. He was holding a coffee cup in his hand. I think the stylist had given him something to drink, so I asked him, "What do you have in the cup?" He looked in, looked back at me, and said, "My identity."

Willie used to have a very fluid identity. When he was little, he would change his last name periodically, becoming a member of different families. At one time, he would be a Smith, happy to be his father's son. The next year, he would become a Zimmerman, identifying with my husband, his stepsisters, and their relatives. Later, he would become a Larsen, a brother to his best friend. There were times he was a Kimball, a Mariani, a Thompson. I used to fret about all this shifting of his identity, but a psychologist told me not to worry; he would settle down. It was when my father died five years ago; he became solidly a Hamilton-Smith, identifying with my family, his grandfather, and all of his cousins in that line and also with his own father again. Since then, he declared that all the other of his identities were wrong and that he had made "a big mistake." The one identity he would never pick up, however, is a young man with Down syndrome. "No, Mom," he says, "I am just like I am."

Erik Erikson, the famous developmental psychologist, says that our "sense of identity provides the ability to experience one's self as something that has continuity and sameness, and to act accordingly."[2] Identity is a good thing. It organizes the psyche, creates coherence in our story, and helps us filter experience. Without it, we would be incredibly disoriented. It would be like channel surfing on cable endlessly without knowing what kind of programs you actually like.

I remember a time in adolescence when I was highly unsure of who and what I was. Seven of my friends had died in a few short months. Everything I thought my life was about was cast into doubt. The reality of death compelled me to change who I thought I was, but this meant throwing off the preferences of my parents—their tastes, some of their values, and things they wanted me to do. I had to consider at a deep level what dying had to do with living, and going to law school wasn't going to do it for me. I didn't have a clear direction. I felt different, alone, and awkward. It seemed like all I had were my questions. It was scary to be without the references points that had held me growing up.

Looking back at this identity crisis through a developmental prism reveals that I was not so special. Apparently, in the process of becoming an adult, we often ask these questions: Who am I? What do I care about? What do I want to do in this life? What matters to me? We define our interests, our likes and dislikes, our deepest values, and how we are going to spend our time and with whom. Granted, there may be privilege in having an identity crisis. It implies the possibility to differentiate from the culture we grew up in, make independent choices, and change. There may be places in the world where perhaps this autonomy from local culture and history doesn't exist. Maybe you can't afford a plane ticket. Maybe if you left, your mother and sisters would suffer without money and a male to look after them. Maybe you did leave to attend college in the West, but went back home to the church or mosque of your youth, just because it felt right.

I don't think we can underestimate the power of ethnocentric identity. To identify with your family, clan, nation, or religion is to belong to something greater than yourself. It is to have a coherent story, tied to the place you grew up, to the people and all the events you all share in common. It is to care about something bigger than yourself. It is to be loyal, faithful to your own kind, and to take your obligations seriously. These are not small things. It is the part of our identity that, when we are threatened, offers the most protection and safety. And make no mistake: under threat, the ethnocentric part of us will do its part to protect our own.

I recall an evening at my house some years ago when two friends came over to a party I was hosting. Both were Americans. One was Jewish, living in Israel for the last twenty years. The other lived in the States, and her family was Palestinian. Her father had been forced to leave Israel after the Six Days War in 1967, and he settled and raised his family in America. I wasn't concerned about the difference when I invited them over. I knew them both well. They had both traveled the world, were highly educated, and believed in love and peace.

By the time the night was over, though, I had felt just how deep the hostility between them was, and they had only just met. I am sure part of it was personal; they just didn't like each other. But identity is not held solely within the individual; it is passed through the body, the memory, and the DNA. When your families have a long history of hating each other for good reason, identity is deep and embedded. And when the ethnocentric identity is activated, kind of like a software program that is running, there is no room for neutrality on the part of your friends or for seeing both points of view, for that matter. These are scenarios in which people's lives and the lives of their families are at stake, so it is a "you are either for us or against us" proposition. And we have to take it seriously.

And yet, "You don't get nowhere hating." I heard an old, black man named Daddy Bruce, who ran a rib place in the outskirts of Denver, say it this way. He opened up every Thanksgiving and fed anyone who wanted to eat. He probably didn't think about identity politics too much, but I'm sure he suffered the wear and tear of prejudice and injustice his whole life. When I was introduced to him, he was at the point he just wanted to feed people.

Sometimes ethnocentric identity is not all it is cracked up to be. The very thing that creates the safety creates the suffering. And sometimes you can't get out of it. When I used to travel in Europe when I was young, people loved the Americans. Now, not so much. Personally, I don't want to stand in as a symbol of global arrogance and greed, but what can I do—say I'm Canadian? Identity is projected onto us as well as inhabited by us. I remember a story of an old Zen master who was mistaken for a thief. A crowd surrounded him and started beating him up. He just took it. When they asked him why he didn't protest, he said he knew they wouldn't be persuaded it wasn't him, so he just waited till it was over.[3] That seems to be part of the predicament. Can you imagine how many times Daddy Bruce didn't want to be looked down upon by white people when he was a black kid growing up in Denver? Identity is not entirely a choice.

And yet somehow he broke free. Claiming a world-centric identity frees us up from the binary bind that ethnocentrism sets up. It allows us to identify as human, instead of with our group. It gives us the opportunity to forgive, to move on, to be free of historical patterns and family insanity. People often move to a world-centric identity because the pain and dilemmas that circulate at ethnocentrism are too much to bear. So they leave home; they leave the church; they get out of the family business. They leave their parents sitting in front of the TV watching FOX news. And then they deal with the sadness and feelings of disloyalty that this change implies. They feel relieved and unburdened. Sometimes when doing my work, it is a challenge to invite people to even take a look at their ethnocentric identities. They want nothing to do with them. Is an identity still there, even if you want nothing to do with it?

Hence, world-centric. I think a world-centric identity is almost more a lifestyle than a psychophysical phenomenon. It helps to have education. It helps to travel. It helps to own a business that buys and sells globally. Or to have a gay child, or to live next door to a Muslim or Jewish or Buddhist family whom you admire. World-centric identity is much more fluid than ethnocentric identity is. People shift meaning from their family of origin to their profession, from religion to political causes, from sports teams to love of animals and the planet. Things change. The world gets bigger. Identity itself starts to become something you do feel free to shape or design. We start to appreciate that we aren't as fixed as we thought.

One afternoon in winter, my husband and I were walking to see the Van Gogh museum in Amsterdam. It was cold and dark, the way it is in northern Europe in January. We were walking like two soldiers off to the front. Our hands were stuffed deep in our pockets, heads down braced against the wind. It was like we were carrying the burden of battle in winter, of rifles and potential mortar fire. I suddenly said to him, "I feel like we are marching toward Russia. Let's change our attitude, and become happy Taoist sages in China on the way to see our beloved master. Even though it is winter, we know when we find him, he will brew hot tea for us and ask us about our journey." Suddenly there was a lift in my step. Some happiness overcame me; my heavy army boots became the light footwear of a devoted disciple.

It sounds like superficial theater, but it is profound, really, that identity can shift. And when it shifts, we can see how sometimes our attachment to it limits us or separates us from the moment and from each other. As Erik Erikson said, identity allows us to experience ourselves with continuity and sameness. But it also creates difference and draws a line in the sand between us and them, and you and me.

To be free of the barrier of identity is a state that happens all the time. It happens when we are fully engrossed in a project, and time flies by. It happens when we are lost deep in the plot of a movie. It happens on a superb ski day when the powder is fine and, because there is no one there to talk to about it, we simply experience it. Any time we are fully aware of this moment, so absorbed by it that our mind is free of self-referencing, identity sleeps. Like it does when we fall into a deep sleep. The world continues without it. There is a Zen expression: "The geese have no mind to cast their shadow. The lake has no mind to receive their image." Birds pass overhead; the weather changes; the light shifts. Everything is as it is, and no one had to work to make it happen.

It is obvious that the effort put forth by the separate self is, at some level, unnecessary. It is like slinging an extra, awkward piece of luggage over our shoulder when both hands are already full. When the hard and fast attachment of identity is set down, attention can be open and relaxed; we become free to participate in the specificity of this very moment and in the details of our life. Or as Zen Master Dōgen said, "To be actualized by the myriad things."[4] In other words, each of us exists in complete relationship to all things, and we are enlivened, shaped, and, you might even say, evoked by everything around us. I don't need "Diane" to be present. In fact, she often just gets in the way. There can be an experience without a story of the self, free of reference points to the past. And without the story, we just might feel free to act naturally, spontaneously, even joyfully.

One of my favorite stories from the Zen tradition is about Bodhidharma, the first Chinese ancestor, and his encounter with the powerful Emperor Wu.[5]

> *Attention! Emperor Wu of Ryo asked the great*
> *master Bodhidharma, "What is the ultimate*
> *meaning of the holy truth of Buddhism?"*
> *Bodhidharma replied, "Vast emptiness. No*
> *Holiness."*
> *The Emperor asked, "Who stands here before me?"*
> *Bodhidharma replied, "I don't know."*

EVER-PRESENT AWARENESS

Ever-present awareness is our true identity. It doesn't change with circumstance or culture or even personal development. Awareness in this moment integrates everything without any effort. Differences arise and dissolve. Emotions come and go. They arise perfectly and dissolve in this open field of presence. Identities also arise, enact their role, and fade away. Bodhidharma leaves the emperor's court and goes away to sit for nine years facing a wall. Every night when we fall into a deep sleep, our identities—all of them—disappear. When we discover, through meditation, what some call "basic goodness," or "True Nature," it relaxes our grip on identity. There's a quality of relaxation and, like Bodhidharma, we have some faith in not knowing who we truly are.

I once asked a group of students to tell me what they understood by the word "enlightenment." To explore the question, I posed a scenario to them. Suppose you were together at a small gathering somewhere, and a new person walked into this room. Someone leaned over to you, pointed to her, and said, "She is enlightened." Any Zen student who has practiced for a while would recoil at the thought of this, but I asked them to try it on, just as a thought experiment.

So I asked, "What qualities would you see from the outside?" Each student had a slightly different, but interesting, response. They didn't remark on who the student's teacher was, how long the student had meditated without interruption, and in which cave the student had sat alone facing the wall. They just described how they imagined the person would be. The first student said it meant that the person would be open and curious, taking in the full detail of each moment. The second student imagined a clarity of mind, free of undue doubt, confusion, and judgments. A third student said that the person would be free and spontaneous, with a lightness of being and able to express joy. A fourth imagined that the student must be compassionate toward others. Finally, the last student said the enlightened student could appreciate the unfolding of life, with its pain and struggles, its disappointments and injuries. The point is that not one of these descriptions requires much of an identity of any kind. In fact, forming a self-identity around any of these characteristics would only get in the way. It is far better to have other people whisper about your charity or kindness than to seek it. Keeping in mind that these virtues can be expressed through robes, business suits, leather jackets, or heels. They can be expressed in any tongue, and received in any language. The human heart is universal, beyond the limits of identity.

THE PRACTICE

1. Remember a time when you lost your identity and it was painful.

2. Now think of a time when you have been free of identity.

3. What is the difference in those two experiences?

NATURAL COMPASSION

When I was a boy and I would see scary things in the news, my mother would say to me, "Look for the helpers. There is always someone who is helping."

—FRED ROGERS[1]

A friend of mine was struggling with some difficult issues in her life, so she stayed up all night praying and contemplating her questions. The next day, her eight-year-old son strolled through the kitchen and with the lisp of an innocent child said, "I'm exhausted."

She asked, "Why, Bjorn?"

"You know," he said, "Dad's been sick. So I took him five limeades and a blanket; then I sat with him for a while and held his hand." As her son was leaving the room, he tossed a smile back over his shoulder and added, "But I'm really happy."

She asked, "Why does helping Dad make you happy?"

Her son got very serious and asked her to sit down. "Mom," he said, "the world is a violent place, and the world is violent because we think so much about ourselves." And then he went on, "So, it's like if you are really thirsty, and you haven't had a drink for a long time, and then someone gives you a big glass of water, it's just really refreshing."

These are the kinds of experiences parents have when their children deliver wisdom beyond their years. My friend interpreted this moment with her son as a response to her questions from the night before. Bjorn was eight, but Bjorn was right. It is refreshing to receive and refreshing to respond with compassion—to your family, to your friends, to the people you encounter throughout the day. It also refreshing to have compassion for the world, and for politics, the media, the crises of our time, and the impermanence of our existence. Most importantly, we must have compassion for ourselves. Without it, we cannot truly offer it to others.

"Compassion" is a deep word. It is a natural outcome of waking up. As our awareness opens to include more, our heart naturally expands. We feel deeply for the suffering and challenges of others—those who are like us and those who are different than we are. A friend of mine, Cindy Wigglesworth,[2] refers to her understanding of compassion as "empathy without a distress signal."[3] A heart filled with compassion can be present to the suffering of others, helping to alleviate it when possible, without undue stress or anxiety coursing through our system.

Bjorn was saying something true to his mother, something real. He sees suffering in the world like the Buddha himself did. When Siddhartha ventured beyond the palace gates, he looked around and saw sickness, old age, and death. These encounters provoked his spiritual search. Then he spent significant time looking deeply into his own being and discovering the pristine, unconditioned nature of his being and consequently, of all beings. He returned to his life with an open heart—a heart moved to respond to the suffering of others.

Like Buddha, we must clarify our mind because often our compassion is born of anxiety rather than relaxation. Sometimes we help others to alleviate our own worry or to comfort ourselves. It is distressing to be faced with suffering; we really would prefer it to go away. So we help others to make ourselves feel better.

Sometimes, we view the other person as a project, as someone who needs healing or fixing. So we are just doing our job when we help out. Like the old adage goes, "When you are a hammer, everything starts to look like a nail." Some of us will go so far as to make martyrs of ourselves, depleting our own energy while enabling others in their addictions or bad behavior because it is so difficult to simply allow their pain to be part of our experience. I have noticed that I struggle most when I encounter young people who are struggling. I want to help them out just to relieve my own anxiety.

If we look closely, we may notice a subtle expectation that accompanies our offer to help. For example, "I will help you, but I want something in return." Perhaps I want to be thanked or acknowledged for what a giving person I am. Maybe I will offer help, but you had better well accept it; otherwise, it is a waste of my time, and we can't have that. Or perhaps there is an underlying quid pro quo. I'll help you as long as you help me the next time I need it. There isn't anything wrong with exchange; giving and receiving are as natural to us as breathing. But when our expectations are unfulfilled, are we still compassionate? Is our heart open? Are we still happy to have responded? Or is our generosity about getting something in return? Is our compassion really an attempt to feel good about ourselves?

WISDOM AND COMPASSION

The Buddhist figure of the bodhisattva of compassion, Avalokiteshvara, is sometimes featured with a thousand arms and hands.[4] In the palm of each hand is an eye. This is a wisdom eye, which symbolizes seeing the situation clearly, being one with it, and acting in accordance with what is needed for the well-being of the whole. It is not that the self is entirely excluded; sometimes we must consider our own well-being when we act. But there are so many occasions when activity simply flows with no self-referencing at all.

Wisdom is the clarity to see what to offer in each moment, without an attachment to how it is supposed to look or what I am going to get for it. In one moment, it is simply being present; in the next, pitching in to do the dishes. And in the next moment, it is working diligently on environmental policy. Then, rolling around on the floor with a child. Sometimes compassion takes the form of a boundary, a limit, or some tough love. I have to say no sometimes to my children, and I don't like feeling their disappointment.

I believe compassion, at its best, is simply doing what needs doing. I was busy loading furniture onto a trailer the other day, and my nephew was helping me. As we were finishing, he picked up a broom and quickly swept out the garage. Not because anyone asked him to, but because there was dirt on the floor, a bunch of dead insects, a free moment, and a broom. He just did what needed doing. This is the freely functioning quality of compassion, which simply gives what the situation asks for.

It reminded me of another time in my life when this nephew's father, my brother, helped me out unexpectedly. I was a single mother at the time, taking care of a small house and yard by myself. It was spring, and I had been away for the weekend. When I returned on Sunday, my brother had come to my house and had cleaned up my entire yard from the wear of winter. He had raked the lawn, trimmed all the trees and bushes, and when I pulled up, he was hauling a huge load of branches over his shoulder to his truck. I remember being in awe of his strength, his robust beauty, and his care for me. I will never forget that day. Of course, I thanked him, but he wasn't looking for anything from me.

GIVE AND TAKE

When we are identified with an open heart, giving and receiving are not separate. It is not like a typical transaction because we receive through the very act of giving. We are completely freed from expecting something in return. There is a very natural exchange in the moment, and even if it involves hauling off a load of branches, it doesn't have the quality of heavy lifting. The great Sufi poet Hafiz wrote, "The earth never says to the sun, you owe me."[5] In time, we are like a shining sun because that is just what we do. Our life is one of spontaneous giving because that is actually all there is to do. Since we are not so concerned with satisfying the needs of the ego, we don't have a "do-gooder" attitude. We are just helpful. We help out this world because it is our world. We care for others because they are not separate from us.

From the perspective of natural compassion, a simple question goes a long way. "Can I be helpful?" is as direct as it is clarifying. And so is trusting someone's response. There can be something very straightforward about it. We have faith in the situation, faith in our question, faith in the other person and that person's capacity to express himself or herself. If somebody doesn't want our help, saying no is a most worthy response.

When there is nothing to be done, we can just sit with someone who is in pain and not have to try to fix it. We can even be in the presence of someone who is dying. What can you do for someone who is on their last legs except be there? Small acts may be in order, like putting a warm cloth on the person's head or helping him or her to the toilet. But it is sufficient to be present to the physical or emotional challenges without feeling the anxiety of needing to make things better. Simple presence is, by itself, deeply comforting. Embodying compassion, we can see things as they are and allow them to be. By allowing things as they are, we may help the other person to allow them, too.

SKILLS

Compassion is an emotion; it is also a state of being. Most importantly, compassion is activity—the embodied gestures of an awakened heart. Sometimes—let's be honest—it helps to have a skill set. Anyone can open a door for another person, and we can all bring someone a cool glass of water when it is hot or a blanket when the sun goes down. But to fill a cavity in a tooth requires dental skills. To mediate a dispute requires good listening and negotiation skills. And to make delicious food requires a certain genius.

In our Zen retreats, we have an exceptionally gifted chef, Julia. She has always been a remarkable cook; she says she learned it from her mother, who was also a natural in her overflowing kitchen. But Julia went on to be trained at the Culinary Institute of America, and her relationship to food has many dimensions. She knows her kitchen tools and how to use them. She understands chemistry and the effects of heat. She is a power shopper at the grocery store, buying the freshest ingredients for the best price. She is a good manager of people and budgets. Her nose and taste buds are extraordinary, and she knows the nutritional value of everything she prepares. Her cooking is the act of a true magician. It is superb, and her very presence is the essence of the word "hospitality." I could go on and on about her, but the point is that compassion is served by developing our skills. And believe me, good food on a meditation retreat is compassion. When the food is good, the people are happy. Julia says that to be a good cook, you have to pay attention, practice, and be open to feedback. This is true of any relationship.

Once I watched an organization of Zen teachers struggle with an ethical issue. They were committed, mature practitioners with immensely open hearts. But they weren't making much progress in resolving their issue with another teacher who had breached one of their ethical codes. So they asked my husband, Michael, if he would help out. Michael is a lawyer. He used to be a judge. He has years of training in thinking through ethical matters and reasoning his way to sound conclusions. He is a very good advisor, and I watched how his training helped this group of teachers think through their issue together and finally resolve their dilemma. It seemed that without his help their good-heartedness lacked the precision to create a result. Sometimes compassionate action needs to be channeled through a specific skill set.

COMPASSION FOR ONESELF

Finally, how do we learn to show compassion to ourselves? Many of the people I work with struggle with a highly developed inner critic that takes a toll on their good heart. As part of practice, they need to recognize how tough they are on themselves and try to find a softer, more encouraging approach. I often ask them to listen to that critical voice inside of them and to notice its tone and messages. They are surprised at how harsh that voice can be. Then I ask them to imagine an ideal coach—someone who is kind, yet firm, and totally committed to getting the best from them. I ask them to imagine how that voice would talk to them instead. This is a very revealing practice for some people.

For others, it is very difficult to ask for help. It is innately challenging to feel the vulnerability in wanting help and to acknowledge how much we need others to simply survive. We grow through our relationships, and there is no way we can do it alone. But we pretend we can. We have to come full circle and be the person who sometimes needs help, instead of the one who gives it. Suddenly we see that it is the same help, the same compassion, that everyone needs and deserves. Instead of feeling guilty or needy or unworthy, we can be grateful when someone lends a hand or gives us a leg up. We are all equal in this way. We are eternally the giver and receiver, and as human beings, we are only complete in this back-and-forth.

So Bjorn brings his dad five limeades—count 'em, five—and a blanket, and we give in the ways we do. It is refreshing to give and to receive. We become larger, more available, and kinder. We contribute to the whole of life by infusing attention in this moment, lending a hand in that one, or appreciating another person spontaneously. We're tending the garden of reality. We have an opportunity to contribute and appreciate that opportunity. In so doing, we are the ones who become more beautiful.

The fullest expression of our meditation and relationship skills practice is in the manifestation of compassion, ethical conduct, and love in the world. The love comes in as many different forms as there are people to express it. It is said that an endless display of talents, gifts, and creativity issue from our practice as naturally as ripe fruit falls from a tree. With sufficient commitment and discipline, our qualities and training become our unique gifts, which we offer to the world. The fulfillment of the spiritual path is the full expression of these gifts. Instead of being motivated by lack, we are now moved by our fullness. Instead of striving to be of service, we learn to show up—ready, available, offering our perspective, our heart, and our skills, with no residue. We no longer compete to make a contribution but find our true place in the world as generous and patient people, doing what it is that we do.

In the Buddhist tradition, the bodhisattva is one who is committed to serving the liberation of all beings. Bodhisattvas make a vow not to dwell in a remote cave absorbed in meditation, but to hang in with the persistent challenges of the human experience in the body, in relationship, and in the world's demand for fairness and social justice. We vow to participate until all beings are liberated, which is another way of saying that love, ethics, and compassion become the activity of our life. The Buddha began his spiritual search prompted by suffering. He culminated it with this simple understanding of the role of love and of kindness:

> *So with a boundless heart*
> *Should one cherish all living beings*
> *Radiating kindness over the entire world.*[6]

THE PRACTICE

1. For one day, make a point of noting everything you do for someone else.
2. On the second day, make a note of everything that someone else does for you.
3. Now compare notes. Any discoveries?

PRACTICE IS THE WAY

In theory there's no difference between theory
*   and practice.*
In practice there is.

—YOGI BERRA[1]

Practice is an act of vision, of faith, and of desire. It means performing something over and over again, in the face of obstacles and disappointments, to accomplish the goal. Practice is disciplined, persistent, and focused. Like a warrior in battle, one who practices exhibits a constant moving forward once a course of action has been decided upon.[2] The practitioner does not let doubt or fear get in the way of the successful completion of an objective.

I've always wanted to practice like this. But I've never gotten close. I don't have that kind of drive. Or steadfastness. Or that straightforward sense of direction and sequence. My objectives are usually unclear. My routines suck. I try to follow a pattern and inevitably do something else altogether. I was talking with a friend the other day about a trip she took to Italy. She attended an event in which doves were released into the crowd. In the minds of the designers, the doves were supposed to fly elegantly toward an end point, but the birds all scattered instead, alighting in all the wrong places. The crowd began to mutter and stir, looking around. "Fiasco," they muttered to each other. "Fiasco."

My practice is like that, kind of a fiasco. Like the designers, I have a clear idea of how I would like it to be, but the birds are all somewhere else. Still, there is the freedom of the sky, beyond these ideas of mine, this suffering and disappointment.

In the beginning, meditation was an attempt to alleviate my suffering. In a regular dose, repeated again and again and again, it was an antidote to confusion and a troubled heart. I think it worked, but not like I expected. It didn't take away the pain but taught me to sit quietly with it. It eliminated the unnecessary fretting and showed me the beauty of how things come and go—empty, as the masters would say. It showed me that there is more to life than my thoughts about it, that my feelings weren't the full truth, and existence is vast and interconnected, including far more than I imagined. Most importantly, meditation cut through my dualistic orientation and, like the doves flying to just the right place, my desire to move from here to there, to get something I thought I knew about but actually didn't have a clue.

The straightforward approach to practice is worthy. As the Nike ad says, "Just do it." Become still, quiet the mind, sit like the mountain and sky—stable and undivided in the face of everything that comes up. Open to the unpleasant part, the down-in-the-dumps part, the making-mistakes part, the prolonged-aching-in-the-heart part. The not knowing and the bouts of joy. Become one in the same as yourself, or "one with" your life. Be diligent about it. Receive guidance from your teacher. Remember to be grateful.

Not being a very determined, forthright practitioner on my own, I hooked my meditation wagon to my husband's star. He is the one who got up and went to the Zen center every morning for years. I tagged along like a pup who is going where his master is going. My husband is the one who enjoyed the demands of long *sesshins*, persisted with koan study, pushed through personal limits, and went the long haul. He is the one who knew how to get up in the morning, face the cold, meet people in the *zendo*, regardless of mood.

I didn't have his fortitude. But I got up anyway because what I did have was an affection for him, for the questions in my heart, and for sitting still once I got to the zendo. I had been meditating for years, but not at the Zen center. Because of this love, I circled back to the cushion, back to my questions, back to my heart. For a bird, there is no way not to be in the sky. But until you see this, you imagine you could have flown differently and better. The repetition was there, but it was never in a straight line. You just come back and come back again, the way a falcon flies back to the leather-bound wrist or a pigeon turns on its wing, flapping toward home.

My practice in relationship is like this too. It isn't so much a discipline, although at times, it is like that. There are moments when I overcome my preferences, submit to listening when I don't feel like it, or ask a question when I would rather not. But my primary motivation is that I love people and I want to understand. So I repeat listening and remember to seek sameness when my mind is clouded with judgments or to be excited by differences when people start to argue.

Each time I drop my old habits of separation and listen instead, or observe, or let go, I jump the ego boundary and land in new territory. Every time I take in another perspective and genuinely consider it, I find there is room to see more and include more. But it ain't easy. It does require commitment and effort and repetition. My choices often feel wrong, or I feel that I'm not doing it right. Or that if I could just learn the One True Thing, I wouldn't have to deal with the Ten Thousand Other Annoying Things. But of course, I know I have to take risks, try new approaches, do it badly, and deal with the feedback. It won't work to maintain a serene countenance. I have to get real.

Recently, a student came to me very humbled, saying, "I wrote my intention on a postcard: 'I want to learn to stay centered in my relationship, express myself clearly, and keep my heart open.' Then I received a minor criticism from my husband this week, and I went bonkers. My intention went right out the window, along with my sanity and my self-respect. I've been there so many times that I am completely discouraged. I don't think it is possible that I can change." Sounds like a fiasco.

I can relate. It is demoralizing when the old habits of the body and brain hijack our efforts to be calm and open. But I remind her that our fundamental practice is simply being present to everything, including negative emotions and when things go awry, and just seeing it all clearly. So even though my student is discouraged, her innate wakefulness is apparent. When she feels really down, she is capable of noticing its excruciating detail and being humbled. She can pay attention.

In time, she will experience openness itself and the miracle of here-and-now wakefulness. She will be less caught up in the mire of negative emotions and the panic of her nervous system. The emotions will come, and they will go, and she will see them as empty of substance. She isn't going to be totally free of them. But why would she want to be? She is human. But her practice will allow her to see, feel, and trust this innate, ever-present awareness. She will see that the birds are always where they should be, and the sky is like it is, boundless. Her conditioned patterns are her suffering, like mine are mine, and yours are yours. I invited her to include them, to love them, because this practice is love.

THE LONG VIEW

When I was introduced to the work of Ken Wilber in 2004,[3] it changed my view of meditation, as well as my thoughts about interpersonal practice. Before, I had very high expectations for my ability to change my patterns in relationship. Then I started to experience how slowly it happened and how minute changes seem to take great effort. I often felt discouraged and, like my student, thought I would never be able to change enough.

But then I met Ken, and I started thinking about evolution in earnest. I started to picture my life in the story of a universe that is 13.8 billion years old and an earth that is a mere 4.7 billion years old. Compared to that kind of timeline, human beings have been around a very short time.

Carl Sagan suggested that, to contemplate time and evolution, we imagine the timeline of the cosmos condensed into one human calendar year.[4] The Big Bang would happen just after midnight of January 1. By early January, the four fundamental forces are at play and the first elements have formed. But nothing more significant than the swirling of gas and dust occurs until May. Then the Milky Way appears and other galaxies form. Then another long period of deep quiet, and in September, our solar system finally forms. Life emerges a month later. Then more quiet. It isn't until December that we start to see a lot of action on our planet. Early forms of life show up, and on about my birthday, December 16, we see the first worms. On the nineteenth, fish and then vertebrates. In the next few days, the first land plants arrive, then insects, amphibians, trees, and reptiles. Dinosaurs come into the picture around December 24 of the cosmic calendar, and on December 25, enter the mammals. On the twenty-seventh, birds show up, and on the twenty-eighth, the dinosaurs depart and become extinct. Still no humans by December 30. Then on the afternoon of December 31, our ancestors finally appear. Late that night, at about 10:00 p.m., the first *Homo sapiens*; at 11:59 the first cave paintings are etched into rock and 11:59:45 marks the beginning of recorded history. In the last nanoseconds, everything else occurs, including outlawing the slave trade, giving women the right to vote, and putting a man on the moon. So I see now that things take time. I am just a flash of intentionality doing my part in learning how to get along and fly right.

Ken points out that as life evolves, nervous systems become increasingly complex, and the capacity for consciousness and self-awareness also evolves.[5] The marvel of evolution in our lives is to be able to consciously pay attention, to reflect on experience, or to tell the story of our own changes. When we start to see our life as evolution in action, then excitement, passion, and eagerness to grow become part of our everyday experience. It is a beautiful paradox because on the one hand, meditation reveals our True Nature beyond time and space, and on the other hand, we can take the long view of time and find our place in it. We have passion to grow, to participate in the marvel of life, and to experience goodness, truth, and beauty. I would like to encourage you in your practice, and I hope that the world excites you.

POCO A POCO

Meditation takes practice. Relationships take practice. My teacher's teacher used to encourage his students by saying, "*Poco a poco.*" Little by little. Whenever we are consciously aware of whatever we are doing right now, we are practicing. When we lose here-and-now awareness, we are practicing getting lost and then regrouping. But as the old sages say, you cannot get off the path. I can guarantee that you will be discouraged, at times; your best efforts may backfire, and sometimes you will be confused and filled with doubt. But if you are persistent, you will notice change, and you will be glad you kept going. I am sure you will surprise yourself at times with your authenticity and your insight. You will grow to trust yourself more, and because you do, you will be open in a deeper way to others. Most importantly, you will start to see beyond yourself. So be willing to practice in a way that works for you and understand that it is a path, not an outcome. There have been many times when I have failed my practice, but it has never failed me.

THE PRACTICE

1. What practices have you have engaged and succeeded in sustaining in your life?
2. Choose a practice from one of the chapters in this book, and commit to doing it for a full year.

16

TAKING HEART

We think we are different, but we share the same life that teaches us the same lessons of love.

—UNKNOWN

It is an amazing time to be alive. We humans are facing some immense, overwhelming, downright frightening global problems. Climate change probably tops the list, with the large-scale shifts in weather patterns, temperatures, and extreme storms it brings about. These changes are upsetting the balance of delicate ecosystems and threaten many forms of life on the planet.

The glaring problem of poverty and economic injustice hasn't gone away, even in the robust era of capitalism. Unfair financial practices, corrupt economic systems, and greed all play a part in exiling huge numbers of people into substandard living conditions, many without the fundamentals of adequate housing, food, and clean water. The status quo is simply not acceptable for a twenty-first-century global community. Differences between rich and poor may seem ever more unsurmountable, but we have to keep working toward a shared vision of social equity. It is the only right thing to do.

We have an abundance of health and human rights issues to deal with: modern-day slave labor, sex trafficking, and a rampant drug trade. All of these take a huge toll on the health of culture wherever they occur. All you have to do is walk down the street in a neighborhood bereft with addiction, and you can feel the heartache and degradation that accompanies runaway drug use. Not to mention the enormous financial cost of crime that accompany addiction and the impacts of these crimes on law enforcement and an overburdened criminal justice system.

Finally, of all the challenging problems we face, the destructive impact of conflict has to be right at the top of the list. Conflicts erupt in our homes and workplaces, afflict our neighborhoods, break out between tribes and different religious groups, propelling nations headlong into war. The number of people around the world who continue to be injured or killed through violence is staggering. This takes an immeasurable toll on the whole of humanity in terms of stress, emotional trauma, and physical harm to people, as well as the incalculable financial costs of paying for our destructiveness. Some things of immense value, including sacred sites and historical treasures, are lost forever. Given all these consequences, we still can't seem to stop ourselves from going to war.

There are people who would argue that the picture isn't quite so bleak. Some studies say that humans are making progress in learning how to get along.[1] They assert that far fewer people are killed in violent episodes today than at any time in our long history. I believe this is true. I believe we are slowly learning better ways to understand our differences, to deal with our struggles, and to overcome obstacles to getting along. It is obvious we still have a long way to go, and true cooperation is necessary to address the other big problems we face.

Now, as always, is the time to take heart and assume that we can and will learn new ways of coexisting. I see this aspiration in my own students who are interested in learning to work with their differences. Some would like to learn to manage the intensity of emotions; others want to become more courageous in the face of conflict, learning to stay present and standing up for themselves instead of running away. Some want the skills to speak more honestly about their own thoughts and feelings, bringing their vulnerability into the conversation, while others want to listen more generously when others are speaking about theirs.

Of the people I know, more of them than ever are interested in making a contribution to good relationships. They want to learn how to resolve their disputes. Some want to become mediators, peacekeepers, or more effective advocates for social change, while others want to have more freedom and harmony in their relationships. Some simply want to resolve their internal conflicts and experience more inner peace. All of these desires require that we outgrow our deeply held patterns of discrimination, injustice, and oppression.

The good news is that learning to deal with our differences is a surefire way to grow as a human being. We are stretched every time we turn toward our differences instead of away from them. Resolving a conflict creatively is an exercise in growth. It demands we open more fully to another's viewpoint, while at the same time holding our own. Embracing more than one perspective is a complex task for the human mind, and like vigorous exercise for the body, it strengthens our capacity to include bigger, more diverse perspectives and to think outside the box for new ideas. Over time, as we get into shape, we become willing to take on even more perspectives. This enables us to look at our situation from a much greater vantage point.

Relationships will often confront us with the need to change—our communication and coping style, our beliefs about intimacy, even the way we find meaning living in the midst of others, and that is a good thing. Without the struggles in relationship, we won't change our way of being. It doesn't mean that every relationship will work out, but it does mean that we can find new ways of growing together and of deepening the recognition of our commonality.

Fortunately, we are developing more approaches for working constructively with our differences. A lot of work has been done in the fields of communication, negotiation, and creative problem solving. In addition, the popularity of mindfulness practice offers us a discipline for becoming intimate with our own fear, anger, and other emotional states. Sitting meditation can help us retrain our nervous system so that we are less stressed and have the ability to take a breath and to watch the fight, flight, or freeze impulses as they pervade our body. Then we can befriend and transform our emotional states rather than reacting immediately. We can always deepen our listening, and we can bring endless curiosity and creativity to our negotiations.

Indeed, it is possible to develop a positive attitude toward the inevitable challenges in our lives. We can learn to see our conflicts and struggles in relationship as a creative opportunity, as a source of energy and vitality. We can learn to engage others when we might prefer to avoid them. It is possible to develop a repertoire of responses that are adapted to each situation and to access unique ways to capture the energy our differences generate without allowing them to degrade or destroy relationship. We can muster the willingness to face our conflicts and work with them in a manner that is awake, even cheerful, and that brings more depth, authenticity, and care to each other.

Without our personal work, we can't participate in the healthy, invigorated communities that we want them to be. But as each of us increases our capacity to deal constructively with one another, we can contribute to increased capacity in our local neighborhoods and communities. Communities then utilize new ways of working with the tension of our differences and the rifts created by injustice. The social harmony that includes the means to transform conflict is a much more reliable harmony than the one that doesn't.

To the extent we can accomplish this, we do the whole

planet a big favor. We create new grooves in our consciousness and evolve methods and structures that can be relied upon to help us deepen our connections and resolve our disputes with more alacrity and efficiency. Imagine what an enormous contribution these skills will make in addressing the other great challenges we face. We could face problems like climate change, poverty, and human rights abuses because we have learned how to genuinely work with each other—when it is going well and when it isn't. Learning how to use these skills on a personal level contributes significantly to our own inner peace, to our connections, our communities. Most importantly, it is an immeasurable contribution to the shared evolution of human culture and to the lasting recognition of our fundamental unity.

THE PRACTICE

1. Take a moment to reflect on the state of the world as you perceive it.
2. Include those things that get you down.
3. Be sure to include what inspires you, lifts you up, or gives you hope.
4. Notice that your heart is big enough to include both.

17

NOT ONE, NOT TWO

And one by one the nights between our separated
*   cities*
are joined to the night that unites us.

—PABLO NERUDA[1]

The universe is one vast whole. Everything comes from the same unknown source, is made up of the same basic materials, and is held within the same dimensions of time and space. Some people call this great uniformity love.

Out of immense sameness, infinite, extravagant differences mysteriously emerge. Quarks are different from atoms, molecules from cells. Single-celled life-forms are different from plants, plants from animals, animals from human beings. I am different from you, we are different from them, they are different from those other guys. Life builds up difference into enormous complexity. We have to remember that the healthiest ecosystems are those containing the most diversity.[2]

Integration of our differences is a form of health. It is also the root of creativity and aesthetic achievement. Music has a bass line, but melodies are exquisite distinctions. Cooking demands coherence in flavor, but just the right amount of pepper or lemon sparks the palate. Great sports teams play with remarkable harmony, but one player makes a play that people can't quit talking about. The biologists talk about biodiversity as wealth in the natural world, and brain scientists describe differentiation in the brain and the importance of integration. Our lives are one big, beautiful contradiction.

The Zen teacher and scholar Taigen Dan Leighton says, "Prajna (or wisdom) is the essential unity or sameness of all things in the midst of their diversity. All things appear and finally cease, all of us will pass away. In spite of the distinctions we cherish, all people are alike in having fears, needs, and desires, in wanting to love and be loved."[3]

MIND OF TWO

In Zen, we sometimes refer to the dualistic mind. It is the mind of two. It perceives sets of opposites like up and down, here and there, good and bad, you and me. Language is a function of this mind because when we speak or write, we use a subject and an object. "I see you." "You hear me." "I want this." "I don't want that."

Analysis is, itself, the mind of two. It divides, sees, contrasts, distinguishes this from that. I ask my husband, Michael, about how he does his job at the Utah Supreme Court, and he replies, "Through careful analysis."

"The legal system," he explains, "was born from the Enlightenment, from the breakthrough that reason is the best source for truth. We developed the confidence to separate from the authority of the church and to use our objectivity as our guide, instead of religious dogma. Our legal system is based on reason and confidence in the power of objectivity."

Remember that to be objective, you have to step away from the subject, be apart from it. To see things clearly and accurately, a judge needs to maintain distance from the prosecutor and the defendant. Judges don't talk about cases with lawyers; sometimes they stay away from social events in order to maintain the right proximity required by their role.

My husband tells me that the practice of law is, at its root, a form of analysis. It involves thinking, discriminating, distinguishing this from that, as well as looking for patterns of sameness, for trends and similarities in cases. There are multitudes of divisions, such as the prosecution and defense. Falsehoods and facts. For and against. You want to win when you present to the Supreme Court; you don't want to lose.

Science is also based on the mind of two. Science observes, divides, and measures. Mathematics divides into smaller and smaller increments. Some people say that physics is measurement. As the resolution of our measurements becomes finer and finer, the rules seem to change. In Newtonian physics, you can still experience an observer separate from phenomena, but when quantum physics comes along, we start to see the way in which there is no real separation; we see subject and object influencing each other. Another shift comes along with string theory. The increments are so small and the divisions so complex that you can no longer use the current techniques and tools of science to validate string theory.

There is a funny clip on YouTube[4] of Brian Greene, the famous mathematician and physicist, arguing with Neil deGrasse Tyson, the celebrity astrophysicist. They are debating whether mathematics really is the language of the universe. Greene proposes the thought experiment of imagining some time in the future. An alien race comes along and says, "Show us what you have done with your math." So we show them, and they say, "Oh that, we tried that, and it will only take you so far." And Neil deGrasse Tyson laughs and says, "Just because you can't prove your string theory, don't blame it on me! Until the day comes when those aliens show us a new language, the math we have, which we made up in our own human brains, is good enough for me."

Maybe the reason math can only take us so far is because division is infinite. Even science, which seems to seek unification, a theory of everything, uses a method that can only disprove hypotheses, leaving an infinite number of untested alternatives. This can only take us so far, always in the direction of difference. These differences are extraordinary; the more of them we discover, the more astonishing the achievements of the modern world—from diseases cured to technologies that transform the way we do business and communicate. All creativity is born of the tension of difference. But we won't discover unity, and certainly not peace, through the mind that divides. We can get closer and closer, but there will always be a gap. Utterly minute, but a gap nonetheless. In order to discover unity and to inhabit peace, we have to relinquish the dividing mind and discover the mind of sameness, the mind of one.

MIND OF ONE

The third Chinese Zen patriarch Chien-chih Seng-ts'an says, "The Great Way is not difficult for those not attached to preferences. When neither love nor hate arises, all is clear and undisguised. Separate by the smallest amount, however, and you are as far from it as heaven is from earth."[5] In the opening lines of his famous discourse, he points to the realization of One Mind. Meditation is the tried-and-true access point for discovering this wholeness, this sameness with all things. Even the word "sameness" is itself a division. Calling something the same doesn't bring us any closer to experiencing it.

But when we sit still, we quiet the language function of the mind and stop the internal talk. We stop dividing reality with our concepts, our preferences, and our evaluations of good and bad. We just sit still. In time, absorbed in stillness, we start to feel at ease. Relaxation penetrates the nervous system; a sense of calm, peace, and expansiveness pervades. Our body, mind, and environment function as one thing—just as they always have, though we didn't see it that way. Now we see that all things belong together because they do. Everything is as it is, and the meditator is the same with it, or even better, *as it*.

There are other methods besides meditation that give us a taste of this essential unity: rocking a baby quietly to sleep, stroking the belly of a loyal pet, watching as the sleek evening sun fades over the dark edge of the horizon. High-performance athletics, gazing at the planet from space, sex, in the moment of merging, are this. Two in excitement, one in surrender, then two in reaching for a cigarette.

I used to have a dog who liked to look deeply into my eyes. One time, he lay on the floor across the room from me after we returned from a winter's hike. We looked at each other; then he held my gaze steady for almost half an hour. There was no action in his gaze, no wanting or questioning. He was just meeting me beyond thought in full presence. In this animal-to-human eye gazing, there was no ultimate difference between us, just an emptiness of identity in the fullness of the moment. I can try to describe this experience to you, but my description is still miles away from what it was like to be with him then. He has since died. I miss his long, steady gaze and dark brown eyes.

Our differences are exciting and often painful. The Buddha said that the mind that separates is the source of our suffering. He observed that in forming an idea of self and other, the mind of two divides us from reality and sets us apart. This separation prevents us from being fully at peace because with self-identity comes a plethora of preferences. We want to be high, not low. We want to be rich, not poor. We want to be in, not out. Where there is a self, there is a good day and a bad day, a success and a failure. This valuing of one side of reality over the other further intensifies separation. It is not that self-concept and self-image are wrong or bad. But they are separating. And without penetrating this separation, we suffer it.

As the mind of two, there are always evaluations, always questions like "Am I good enough, smart enough, attractive enough?" There will always be comparisons and unconscious forms of competition. We think the self can get it right, if we work hard enough. And there is satisfaction in working hard, in accomplishing things, and in achieving mastery. But serenity and deep satisfaction involve relaxing the self-concept, the comparisons, and the idea of always gaining more. Also, we have a modern notion that there is courage in our separation and individualism. I believe there is bravery in the willingness to be alone. But let's be clear that solitude is only satisfying when we find oneness with ourselves and our environment. Without the recognition of our deep connection, aloneness is lonely, stressful, and isolating. After a long period of being alone, rather than radiating the deep peace of the contemplative, you might end up ranting and raving like a backwoods hermit. There is a big difference.

Conflict is the most extreme form of difference. Hatred is the emotion of extreme judgment. Violence is the attempt to annihilate difference. The mind of two is involved in every brawl because a conflict requires difference. There has to be an other side or an enemy. So do not ask the mind of two to be at peace. That is not its nature. It is dynamic and creative, full of change and disruption.

Differences have to be worked with, acknowledged, soothed, integrated. We can work with them by discovering the layer of sameness and commonality in human community. We may find even deeper resolution and unity with all that is. The Bible says, "Make my joy complete by being of the same mind, maintaining the same love, united in spirit, intent on one purpose."[6] Zen Master Dōgen says, "The mind is no other than mountains and rivers, and the earth; the mind is the sun, the moon, and stars."[7] So the trick is to discover the sameness that pervades and includes our differences and unity in the details of our everyday life.

NOT ONE, NOT TWO

I have been describing the mind of one and the mind of two, but this distinction is a mental device, something the mind and language perform together. We make a profound distinction in an effort to see more clearly, to understand more fully. To some degree it helps. In another way, not at all. Because the lived experience is not of one, nor two: not of sameness nor difference. It is immediate, thorough, and intimate.

There is a beautiful moment in Zen lore called "Zhaozhou's Deeply Secret Mind":[8]

> A nun asked Master Zhaozhou Congshen, "What is
>   the deeply secret mind?"
> Zhaozhou squeezed her hand.
> The nun said, "Do you still have this?"
> Zhaozhou said, "You are the one who has this."

This is a conversation, a moment of deep contact and love. Love is the thing that is most profound, transcending one and two, containing all of our contradictions. When our heart is open, it is vast. The sameness, the deep secret between us, is expressed completely through our differences. Without them, she wouldn't have her question. Without them, he wouldn't reach out and touch her hand.

She says, "Do you have it?"

He says, "You do."

THE PRACTICE

1. Consider the word "intimacy." What is most intimate for you in this moment?

Epilogue

Sometimes people ask me why I choose to practice Zen. Like Bodhidharma, one answer is "I don't know." Another one is that I love the meditation, the stories, and the poems from this profound tradition. Please enjoy this one. It is chanted every morning in Zen temples and meditation centers all over the world. It was the inspiration for this book.

Harmony of Difference and Sameness[1]

SHITOU XIQIAN, 700–790
(SEKITO KISEN)

The mind of the great sage of India
is intimately communicated from west to east.
While human faculties are sharp or dull,
The Way has no northern or southern ancestors.
The spiritual source shines clear in the light;
the branching streams flow on in the dark.
Grasping at things is surely delusion;

according with sameness is still not enlightenment.
All the objects of the senses
interact and yet do not.
Interacting brings involvement.
Otherwise, each keeps its place.
Sights vary in quality and form,
sounds differ as pleasing or harsh.
Refined and common speech come together in
    the dark,
clear and murky phrases are distinguished in
    the light.
The four elements return to their natures
just as a child turns to its mother.
Fire heats, wind moves,
water wets, earth is solid.
Eye and sights, ear and sounds,
nose and smells, tongue and tastes;
Thus with each and every thing,
depending on these roots, the leaves spread forth.
Trunk and branches share the essence;
revered and common, each has its speech.
In the light there is darkness,
but don't take it as darkness;
In the dark there is light,
but don't see it as light.

Light and darkness oppose one another
like front and back foot in walking.
Each of the myriad things has its merit,
expressed according to function and place.
Phenomena exist; box and lid fit.
Principle responds; arrow points meet.
Hearing the words, understand the meaning;
don't set up standards of your own.
If you don't understand the Way right before you,
how will you know the path as you walk?
Progress is not a matter of far or near,
but if you are confused, mountains and rivers block
    your way.
I respectfully urge you who study the mystery,
do not pass your days and nights in vain.

Notes

Preface

1. Diane Musho Hamilton, *Everything Is Workable: A Zen Approach to Conflict Resolution* (Boston: Shambhala Publications, 2013).

CHAPTER 1: *Same and Different*

1. Zen Master Mumon, *The Gateless Gate*, trans. Zenkei Shibayama (Boston: Shambhala Publications, 1974), 331.
2. Martin Fischer, Howard Douglas Fabing, and Ray Marr, *Fischerisms: Being a Sheaf of Sundry and Divers Utterances Culled from the Lectures of Martin H. Fischer, Professor of Physiology in the University of Cincinnati* (Springfield, IL: C.C. Thomas, 1937).
3. Edward O. Wilson, *The Social Conquest of Earth* (New York: Liveright Publishing, 2012).
4. David Schiller, *The Little Zen Companion* (New York: Workman Publishing, 1994), 55.

CHAPTER 2: *Together, Then Apart*

1. Erik H. Erikson, *Identity: Youth and Crisis* (New York: W. W. Norton & Co., 1994).
2. Erik H. Erikson and Robert Coles, *The Erik Erikson Reader* (New York: W. W. Norton & Co., 2001).
3. Jean Piaget and Bärbel Inhelder, *The Psychology of the Child* (New York: Basic Books, 1969).

CHAPTER 3: *The Ego Divides*

1. Chögyam Trungpa and Carolyn Rose Gimian, *The Essential Chögyam Trungpa* (Boston: Shambhala Publications, 1999), 41.

2. Shelley H. Carson and Ellen J. Langer, "Mindfulness and Self-Acceptance," *Journal of Rational-Emotive & Cognitive-Behavior Therapy* 24, 1 (2006): 30.

3. Bessel Van Der Kolk, *The Body Keeps the Score* (New York: Viking, 2014), 60.

4. Daniel Goleman, *Emotional Intelligence: Why It Can Matter More Than IQ* (New York: Bantam, 1996), 14.

5. Jon Kabat-Zinn, *Full Catastrophe Living* (New York: Dell, 1990), 20.

6. Diane Musho Hamilton, *Everything is Workable: A Zen Approach to Conflict Resolution* (Boston: Shambhala Publications, 2013), 39.

7. Alan Watkins, *Coherence* (London: Kogan Page, 2014), 67–68.

CHAPTER 4: *Mindfulness and Meditation*

1. Sharon Salzberg, *Real Happiness: Learn the Power of Meditation: A 28-Day Program* (New York: Workman Publishing, 2010), 104.

2. Daphne M. Davis and Jeffrey A. Hayes, "What Are the Benefits of Mindfulness? A Practice Review of Psychotherapy-Related Research," *Psychotherapy* 48, 2 (2011): 198–208.

3. Jon Kabat-Zinn, https://en.wikipedia.org/wiki/Jon_Kabat-Zinn. Suggested reference to book instead of Wikipedia: Jon Kabat-Zinn, *Full Catastrophe Living: Using the Wisdom of Your Body and Mind to Face Stress, Pain, and Illness* (New York: Dell, 1991).

4. Leonard L. Riskin and Rachel Wohl, "Mindfulness in the Heat of Conflict: Taking Stock," *Harvard Negotiation Law Review* 20 (May 2015): 121.

CHAPTER 5: *Listening: The Supreme Skill*

1. Brian Eno, "Brian Eno Interview" by Franck Mallet, *Artpress*, issue 271, September 2001, http://music.hyperreal.org/artists/brian_eno/interviews/artpress01.html (accessed March 24, 2016).

2. Jalāl al-Dīn Rūmī and Coleman Barks, *The Essential Rumi* (Edison, NJ: Castle Books, 1997), 36.

CHAPTER 6: *Expressing Our Uniqueness*

1. Bruce Lee and John Little, *Striking Thoughts: Bruce Lee's Wisdom for Daily Living* (North Clarendon, VT: Tuttle Publishing, 2002), 173.

2. Agnes De Mille, *Martha: The Life and Work of Martha Graham: A Biography* (New York: Random House, 1991), 264.

3. David Schiller, *The Little Zen Companion* (New York: Workman Publishing, 1994), 4.

4. Marshall Rosenberg, *Nonviolent Communication: A Language of Life* (Encinitas, CA: Puddledancer Press, 2015).

5. *I Have a Dream: The Story of Martin Luther King in Text and Pictures* (New York: Time-Life Books, 1968).

6. Clarence B. Jones and Stuart Connelly, *Behind the Dream: The Making of the Speech That Transformed the Nation* (New York: St. Martin's Press, 2013), 112–15.

7. Peggy McIntosh, *White Privilege and Male Privilege: A Personal Account of Coming to See Correspondences through Work in Women's Studies* (Wellesley, MA: Wellesley College, Center for Research on Women, 1988).

CHAPTER 7: *Depth of Feeling*

1. Ken Wilber, *Integral Psychology: Consciousness, Spirit, Psychology, Therapy* (Boston: Shambhala Publications, 2000), 12–17.

2. Robert Augustus Masters, *Emotional Intimacy: A Comprehensive Guide for Connecting with the Power of Your Emotions* (Boulder, CO: Sounds True, 2013).

CHAPTER 8: *Talking About Difference: Five Steps*

1. bell hooks, *Killing Rage: Ending Racism* (New York: H. Holt and Co., 1995), 265.

2. Linda Graham, "Oxytocin: Helping the Brain Generate Feelings of Deep Connection and Well Being," *Wise Brain Bulletin* 2, 11 (November 2008): 7.

3. Sarah Klein, "Adrenaline, Cortisol, Norepinephrine: The Three Major Stress Hormones Explained," The Huffington Post, April 17, 2013, www.huffingtonpost.com/2013/04/19/adrenaline-cortisol -stress-hormones_n_3112800.html (accessed July 20, 2016).

CHAPTER 9: *Negotiating with David*

1. David Holladay, *No Man's Land: S1 E1 Adapt or Die*, The History Channel, aired March 9, 2014, www.history.com/shows/no -mans-land/season-1/episode-1 (accessed March 26, 2016).

2. Roger Fisher and William Ury, *Getting to Yes: Negotiating Agreement without Giving In* (Boston: Houghton Mifflin Harcourt, 1986).

CHAPTER 10: *The Great Divide: Conflict*

1. *Monsieur Verdoux*, directed by Charlie Chaplin, performed by Charlie Chaplin (Los Angeles: RBC Films, 1947).

2. Edward Desmond, "Interview with Mother Teresa: A Pencil in the Hand of God," *Time*, December 4, 1989, http://content.time .com/time/magazine/article/0,9171,959149,00.html (accessed March 30, 2016).

CHAPTER 11: *Differences in Style*

1. Charles Bukowski, "Style," *Mockingbird Wish Me Luck* (Santa Rosa, CA: Black Sparrow Press, 1972), 156.
2. Irini Rockwell, *The Five Wisdom Energies: A Buddhist Way of Understanding Personalities, Emotions, and Relationships* (Boston: Shambhala Publications, 2002).
3. Ken Wilber, *The Integral Vision* (Boston: Shambhala Publications, 2007), 45.

CHAPTER 12: *You and Me, Us and Them*

1. Pink Floyd, "Us and Them," *Pulse: The Dark Side of the Moon* (Columbia, 1973), vinyl.
2. Ken Wilber, *Sex, Ecology, and Spirituality* (Boston: Shambhala Publications, 2000), 210.
3. Otto F. Kernberg, *Borderline Conditions and Pathological Narcissism* (New York: J. Aronson, 1975).
4. Susanne R. Cook-Greuter, "Nine Levels of Increasing Embrace in Ego Development: A Full-Spectrum Theory of Vertical Growth and Meaning Making," 2013, prepublication version, www.cook-greuter.com (accessed March 24, 2016).
5. Daniel J. Siegel, *The Developing Mind: How Relationships and the Brain Interact to Shape Who We Are* (New York: Guilford Press, 2015), 9–10.
6. Ken Wilber, *The Collected Works of Ken Wilber, Vol. 8* (Boston: Shambhala Publications, 2000), 47–49.
7. Frank White, *The Overview Effect: Space Exploration and Human Evolution* (Boston: Houghton-Mifflin, 1987).
8. Ken Wilber, *The Integral Vision* (Boston: Shambhala Publications, 2007), 34.

9. Jack Kerouac, *The Dharma Bums* (New York: Penguin Books, 2006), 134.

CHAPTER 13: *Free from Identity*

1. Hui-neng and Thomas F. Cleary, *The Sutra of Hui-neng, Grand Master of Zen: With Hui-neng's Commentary on the Diamond Sutra* (Boston: Shambhala Publications, 1998).
2. Erik H. Erikson, *Childhood and Society* (New York: Norton, 1964), 42.
3. Kazuaki Tanahashi, *Sky Above, Great Wind: The Life and Poetry of Zen Master Ryokan* (Boston: Shambhala Publications, 2012), 4.
4. Dōgen and Kazuaki Tanahashi, *Treasury of the True Dharma Eye: Zen Master Dogen's Shobo Genzo* (Boston: Shambhala, 2010), 30.
5. Gerry Shishin Wick and Zhengjue, *The Book of Equanimity: Illuminating Classic Zen Koans* (Boston: Wisdom Publications, 2005), 13.

CHAPTER 14: *Natural Compassion*

1. Fred Rogers, "Look for the Helpers," www.youtube.com /watch?v=-LGHtc_D328 excerpted from www.youtube.com /watch?v=LnO9voHUi54 (accessed on March 25, 2016).
2. Cindy Wigglesworth, *SQ21: The Twenty-One Skills of Spiritual Intelligence* (Cork: BookBaby, 2012).
3. Richard J. Davidson and Sharon Begley, *The Emotional Life of Your Brain: How Its Unique Patterns Affect the Way You Think, Feel, and Live—and How You Can Change Them* (New York: Hudson Street Press, 2012), 222.
4. Taigen Dan Leighton, *Faces of Compassion: Classic Bodhisattva Archetypes and Their Modern Expression: An Introduction to Mahayana Buddhism* (Boston: Wisdom Publications, 2012), 171.
5. Hafiz, "The Sun Never Says," *The Gift* (New York: Penguin Compass, 1999), 34.
6. "Karaniya Metta Sutta: The Buddha's Words on Loving-Kindness" (Khp 9), translated from the Pali by the Amaravati

Sangha, *Access to Insight (Legacy Edition)*, November 2, 2013, www.accesstoinsight.org/tipitaka/kn/khp/khp.9.amar.html (accessed March 30, 2016).

CHAPTER 15: *Practice Is the Way*

1. Yogi Berra, also attributed to Nassim Nicholas Taleb, *Antifragile: Things That Gain from Disorder* (New York: Random House, 2012), 213. The earliest known appearance of this quote in print is Walter J. Savitch, *Pascal: An Introduction to the Art and Science of Programming* (Menlo Park, CA: Benjamin Cummings Publishing, 1984), where it is attributed as a "remark overheard at a computer science conference." It circulated as an anonymous saying for more than ten years before attributions to Jan L. A. van de Snepscheut and Yogi Berra began to appear (and later still to various others), https://en.wikiquote.org/wiki/Yogi _Berra (accessed March 24, 2016).

2. Daisetz Teitaro Suzuki, *Zen and Japanese Culture* (New York: Pantheon Books, 1959).

3. Ken Wilber, *A Brief History of Everything* (Boston: Shambhala Publications, 1996).

4. "Carl Sagan: The Cosmic Calendar," *Cosmos*, YouTube, 2011, www .youtube.com/watch?v=GzG9fHMr9L4 (accessed March 28, 2016).

5. Ken Wilber, *Integral Psychology: Consciousness, Spirit, Psychology, Therapy* (Boston: Shambhala Publications, 2000), 280.

CHAPTER 16: *Taking Heart*

1. Steven Pinker, *The Better Angels of Our Nature: Why Violence Has Declined* (New York: Penguin Group USA, 2012).

CHAPTER 17: *Not One, Not Two*

1. Pablo Neruda, *The Captain's Verses (Los versos del Capitán)*, trans. Donald Walsh (New York: New Directions Publishing, 1972), 119.

2. James B. Grace, T. Michael Anderson, Eric W. Seabloom, Elizabeth T. Borer, Peter B. Adler, W. Stanley Harpole, Yann Hautier, Helmut Hillebrand, Eric M. Lind, Meelis Pärtel, Jonathan D. Bakker, Yvonne M. Buckley, Michael J. Crawley, Ellen I. Damschen, Kendi F. Davies, Philip A. Fay, Jennifer Firn, Daniel S. Gruner, Andy Hector, Johannes M. H. Knops, Andrew S. Macdougall, Brett A. Melbourne, John W. Morgan, John L. Orrock, Suzanne M. Prober, and Melinda D. Smith, "Integrative Modelling Reveals Mechanisms Linking Productivity and Plant Species Richness," *Nature* 529.7586 (2016): 390-93.

3. Taigen Dan Leighton, *Faces of Compassion* (Boston: Wisdom Publications, 2003), 75.

4. "Neil DeGrasse Tyson Makes Fun of Brian Greene's String Theory," YouTube, 2013, www.youtube.com/watch?v=20yRHABy5Oo (accessed March 29, 2016).

5. Seng-ts'an, Richard B. Clarke, and Gyokusei Jikihara, *Hsin-hsin Ming: Verses on the Faith-Mind* (Buffalo, NY: White Pine Press, 2001), 3.

6. Phil 2:2 NASB.

7. Dōgen and Kazuaki Tanahashi, *Treasury of the True Dharma Eye: Zen Master Dogen's Shobo Genzo* (Boston: Shambhala, 2010), 46.

8. Florence Caplow and Susan Moon, *The Hidden Lamp: Stories from Twenty-Five Centuries of Awakened Women* (Boston: Wisdom Publications, 2013), 104.

EPILOGUE

1. "Harmony of Difference and Sameness," www.sacred-texts.com /bud/zen/sandokai.htm (accessed March 30, 2016).